THE NEW ORLEANS SNIPER

A Phenomenological Case Study of Constituting the Other

Frances Chaput Waksler

University Press of America,® Inc.
Lanham · Boulder · New York · Toronto · Plymouth, UK

Copyright © 2010 by
University Press of America,® Inc.
4501 Forbes Boulevard
Suite 200
Lanham, Maryland 20706
UPA Acquisitions Department (301) 459-3366

Estover Road
Plymouth PL6 7PY
United Kingdom

All rights reserved
Printed in the United States of America
British Library Cataloging in Publication Information Available

Library of Congress Control Number: 2010936059
ISBN: 978-0-7618-5389-3 (paperback : alk. paper)
eISBN: 978-0-7618-5390-9

∞™ The paper used in this publication meets the minimum
requirements of American National Standard for Information
Sciences—Permanence of Paper for Printed Library Materials,
ANSI Z39.48-1992

TO

Professor George Psathas

Professor Erazim Kohák

Professor John Mogey

Professor Julius A. Roth

*with gratitude for the knowledge and
support offered me throughout the years*

Contents

Preface	vii
Acknowledgments	ix
Chapter 1: Introduction	1
The Project	3
The Event	4
The Data	5
Timeline of Key Events	6
Chapter 2: Constituting the Other: The Context	9
The Immediate Context for Assumptions	9
The Power of First Assumptions	12
Chapter 3: Constituting the Other: The Evidence	15
What One Person is Capable of Doing: Mark Essex (The "First" Sniper)	16
Signs of an Other	19
Others are Seeable	19
Others and Their Actions are Hearable	25
Turn-Taking (Reciprocity)	27
Leavings	28
Speculation and Conspiracy Theories	32
What One person is Capable of Doing: The "Escape" of the Second Sniper	34
A Note on Ambiguity: Either/Or Explanations	36
Legitimating Evidence	37
Chapter 4: The Aftermath: Unconstituting the Other	41
Reworking the Evidence	42
NOPD Report	44
What One Person is Capable of Doing: Mark Essex (The "First" Sniper)	47
Reworking Signs of an Other	49
Others are Seeable: Sightings at Howard Johnson's	50
Others are Seeable: Retrospective Sightings	57
Others and Their Actions are Hearable	59
Turn-Taking (Reciprocity)	61
Leavings	63
Speculations and Conspiracy Theories	65
Lingering Traces of a Second Sniper	67
A Path for a Second Sniper	71
Chapter 5: Conclusion	75
Appendix: Witnesses' Sightings and Descriptions of Sniper(s)	79
Bibliography	93
Index	99

PREFACE

In January 1973 I followed with great interest the television news broadcasts of sniping from the Downtown Howard Johnson's Motel in New Orleans and, after the death of the first sniper, the ultimately unsuccessful search for a second sniper. I was just finishing my dissertation, *The Essential Structures of Face-to-Face Interaction: A Phenomenological Analysis*, in which I explored how a person identifies an Other as an *interactional* Other. I immediately saw the New Orleans event as the basis for a case study of that topic: how was a second sniper first identified as an Other and then denied existence—or, as I would say now, first constituted and then unconstituted?

I did not pursue the topic at that time, but the intriguing aspects of the case remained with me. A turning point came in 2002 when, on a whim, I phoned the offices of *The New Orleans Times-Picayune* and spoke with the Head Librarian, Nancy Burris. When I told her of my interest in the sniper case, she said that she would send me an extensive file of clippings from both *The Times-Picayune* and *The New Orleans States-Item* that, given the interest in the event at the time, she had compiled. Data in hand, I was ready to begin.

Over the years, as I was consulting the works of Edmund Husserl for other writing projects, the relevance of his analysis to the sniping event continued to come to mind. Of direct relevance were his discussions of the constitution of the Other, issues that might be demonstrated empirically by the New Orleans sniper data.

> The only conceivable manner in which others can have for me the sense and status of existent others, thus and so determined, consists in their being constituted *in me* as others. If they get that sense and status from sources that yield a continual confirmation, then they do *exist* (as I am *compelled* to say), but exclusively as having the sense with which they are constituted. . .(Fifth Cartesian Meditation, 1960: 128, emphasis in original).

How is such confirmation achieved? When continual confirmation fails, what follows?

With Husserl's texts in one hand and newspaper clippings in the other, I set to work. The sniper data to follow discloses in detail the processes whereby constitution—and, eventually, unconstitution—of an Other can occur.

Frances Chaput Waksler
Cambridge, MA
August 2010

ACKNOWLEDGMENTS

My first debt of gratitude is to Nancy Burris, Head Librarian, *The Times-Picayune* (New Orleans), who provided me extensive newspaper accounts of the event, both contemporaneous and retrospective, as well as assistance throughout the research process. Without her help this project would not have been possible. Irene Wainwright, Archivist, New Orleans Public Library, gave me access to the August 31, 1973 New Orleans Police Department Report, the only available copy since Hurricane Katrina had destroyed the Police Department's copy. Both were gracious as well as efficient. Professors Jeff Coulter and Maxine Sheets-Johnstone read early drafts of the material and provided encouragement. Professor Greg Smith offered useful insights. Professor Kenneth Lieberman urged me forward, imagining what such a book would look like (even to back cover reviews). Two anonymous readers also gave helpful suggestions. I had the opportunity to present portions of this material at the meetings of the Society for Phenomenology and the Human Sciences (Boston, MA 2003) and as a keynote address at the meetings of the International Human Science Research Conference (St. Catharines, Ontario, 2004) organized by Professor Maureen Connolly. Lieutenant Stephen Carrabino of the Somerville, MA Police Department reviewed materials in light of my goal of fairly and sympathetically presenting the police involved in the event and provided help in clarifying some aspects of the police report. Professor Lester Embree offered helpful information when I needed it. Samantha M. Kirk and Brian DeRocco of University Press of America were always available with just the answers I needed. Laura Cherry carefully copy edited the manuscript—not everyone has a poet as a copyeditor. Norman Waksler has lived with this project for many years and read innumerable drafts, keeping a particularly careful eye on my prose style.

Materials from *The Times-Picayune* and *The States Item* © 2010 The Times-Picayune Publishing Co. All rights reserved. Used with permission of *The Times-Picayune*.

Materials from Edmund Husserl, trans. Dorion Cairns, *Cartesian Meditations: An Introduction to Phenomenology* (1960), reprinted by permission of Martinus Nijhoff, The Hague, Netherlands.

CHAPTER 1.
INTRODUCTION

> [W]e generally say, in the case of experiencing a man: the other is himself there before us "in person." On the other hand, this being there in person does not keep us from admitting forthwith that . . . neither the other. . .himself, nor his subjective processes or his appearances themselves, nor anything else belonging to his own essence, becomes given in our experience originally (Husserl, Fifth Cartesian Meditation,[1] 1960: 108–9).

At first sight the *problematic* nature of an Other might appear to be a rare practical matter. Isn't the Other "given" in everyday life experience? When walking in a crowd of people, despite my phenomenological perspective I am likely not to question whether those I am in the midst of are Others. Others are simply and unproblematically there. But then again, I do at times wonder if the assorted sounds in my house at night indicate an intruder. Is there someone there? And yes, I have occasionally spoken to a mannequin[2] in a store and initially been surprised by her "rudeness." Such events may be fleeting, but perhaps in the world of everyday life they are not so rare after all.

Thus I begin with two brief examples of constituting an Other that are in some respects more "ordinary" than that of the New Orleans sniper event, the subject of my analysis here, but that nonetheless display similar problematic aspects. These examples are most instructively seen both from the perspective of the one offering the account as "truth" and from the perspective of a "doubting outsider."

"FANTASY" OTHERS. If children see dolls as real, then children's responses are what one might expect were real Others involved. The following story, taken from my book *The Little Trials of Childhood and Children's Strategies for Dealing with Them* (1996), cannot be appreciated fully unless the reality of dolls as Others is acknowledged. Helen writes,

> When I was 7 I neglected my most prized possession. This is something that I had never done before, and I truly felt terrible about it. My family and I were driving to my aunt and uncle's house in Baltimore, MD. Upon our arrival, I became so excited that on this hot, sunny summer day I threw Judy, my baby jelly doll, in the back of

> the station wagon. I forgot about her. After visiting for a few hours I wanted Judy. . . .My father went out to the car just to make sure that I had not left her there, and sure enough there was Judy. She had melted. I was devastated. I was her 'parent' and I left my 'child' sitting in the back of a station wagon, in the scorching sun. I was hysterical. I 'killed' my child. As I look back on this experience, I still feel horrible (in Waksler, 1996).

That adults might minimize Helen's distress, viewing it as "childish," does not negate her experience of the doll as Other.

SUPERNATURAL OTHERS. Edward Berryman says of his informant Susan, who claims to have apparitions of Jesus, the Virgin Mary and other saintly figures:

> During an interview, Susan told me, 'I see and hear them (Jesus and the Virgin Mary) as I see you now.' Susan also takes pictures of some of her apparitions. As she tells the story, this happens when she is in a state of trance. When she 'awakes' from the apparition she has Polaroid shots around her (personal communication; see also Berryman, 2005).

Observers (outsiders) might have difficult recovering the deities in the photographs, but for Susan they count as clear evidence of her direct experience of supernatural others.

Recognizing the potentially problematic nature of the Other allows for consideration of concrete situations in which the existence of interactionally available Others may be denied: children's imaginary friends, children said to be feral, children themselves, the deaf, the retarded, schizophrenics, animals, guardian angels, demons, and those who have "passed on," to suggest but a few.[3] My concern with the New Orleans sniper is with an Other whose very physical existence as well as interactional availability is problematic.

Upon reflection, in light of the above kind of examples, and in particular with reference to the sniper data to follow here, I have come to see the "problem" of the Other as of broad practical and theoretical relevance. When in everyday life the Other is problematic, face-to-face interaction is compromised, for *inter*action can only occur when each participant takes the Other for an Other. If Otherness is not granted by participants, face-to-face interaction cannot proceed. If Otherness is denied by outside observers of face-to-face interaction, one participant may be faulted as deceived, duped, immature, or mad and the postulated Other participant as imaginary or otherwise dismissed.

Understanding how Others are constituted provides resources for identifying the grounds for claims about those Others. W.I. Thomas' dictum, if people define situations as real they will be real in their consequences, is relevant here. Understanding the resources that people use as they define an Other as an Other provides entrée into their worlds. It is that understanding that I seek in analyzing events surrounding the New Orleans sniper.

THE PROJECT
My goal is to follow Husserl's recommendation to explore *how*, in a given situation, an Other is constituted, *how* people, with their general procedures and resources, use them to constitute an Other in a specific situation—one in which the very existence of that Other is problematic.[4]

> We wish, then, to consider the surrounding life-world concretely, in its neglected relativity and according to all the manners of relativity belonging essentially to it—the world in which we live intuitively, together with its real entities. . .; but [we wish to consider them] *as* they give themselves to us at first in straightforward experience, and even [consider] the ways in which their validity is sometimes in suspense (between being and illusion, etc.) (Husserl, 1970: 156, emphasis in original).[5]

The data I am subjecting to detailed analysis regards what has been generally referred to, both at the time (1973) and afterwards, as "The New Orleans Sniper."[6] That very designation, however, suggests, erroneously, that a single sniper was postulated from the onset of the event. What makes this case particularly fruitful for analysis is the *work* that initially went into determining that there was at least a second sniper involved and the later *work* to conclude, albeit not without dissent, that there had been only one sniper.

My concern is with how that second sniper was first constituted and later unconstituted. What were the concrete elements in the surrounding life-world? How were experiences at the time described? How were "being and illusion" addressed? More specifically, how was *in situ* evidence used to constitute an Other–a second sniper–when the very existence of that Other was problematic and how was that same and new evidence used to unconstitute that Other? If, as Husserl claims in the epigraph, the Other is not given originally, then how? When the Other's very existence is ambiguous, the work of constituting the Other becomes evident. What are the features of that work? Husserl sets forth the *problem* of the Other; the case of the New Orleans Sniper offers an instance where the problematic nature of the Other is central. I hope to show that Husserl's ideas can be directly applied to a particular instance of a problematic Other and can illuminate the intricate processes whereby an Other is constituted.

To give a sense of my project and approach, I begin by juxtaposing a quotation from Edmund Husserl's Second Cartesian Meditation and a newspaper description of the data under consideration here.

Husserl writes,

> What are others, what is the world, for me?—Constituted phenomena, merely something produced within me. Never can I reach the point of ascribing being in the absolute sense to others, any more than to the physical things of Nature, which exist only as transcendentally produced affairs (Second Cartesian Meditation, 1960: 52, footnote).

The Times-Picayune (New Orleans) reports that on Sunday, January 7, 1973, at 10:52 a.m., the first fire alarm sounded from the Downtown Howard Johnson's Motel[7] in New Orleans, Louisiana. A police report issued after the event described the scene that Sunday:

> The number and location of fires on several levels of the motel, the killing committed on different levels, the snipings from various levels, all in combination were sufficient to create a reasonable belief that there was more than one person involved in the acts of killings and arson...(quoted in *The Times-Picayune* (T-P), 2/20/73).

That day, six were reported dead (a seventh died later), ten others wounded. That night at approximately 8:50 p.m., Mark James Essex, shooting from the roof of the hotel, was gunned down by police. After his death, the search continued for "the Other" sniper or snipers.[8] None was ever found or identified and later reports questioned the very existence of that Other (a second sniper).

It is this search for the Other—the second sniper—and the failure to find that Other that is the focus of my analysis. I am guided by Husserl's assertion that

> it is necessary to begin with a systematic explication of the overt and implicit intentionality in which the being of others for me becomes 'made' and explicated in respect of its rightful content—that is, its fulfillment-content (Fifth Cartesian Meditation, 1960: 91–2).

Although in everyday life the Other may routinely be viewed as given, underlying work is necessary to sustain that *given* character. When the Other's very existence is unambiguous, the constitution of that Other is obscured; when the Other's existence (here, a second sniper and thus a *particular* Other) *is* ambiguous, problematic, and consequential, the work of constituting the Other is displayed.

THE EVENT

On Sunday night, January 7, 1973, Mark James Essex, sniping from atop the Downtown Howard Johnson's Motel, 330 Loyola Avenue, New Orleans, Louisiana, was gunned down by police. After his death, the search continued for the other sniper or snipers, as indicated in the following headlines of New Orleans' newspaper stories *after Essex's death*:

> SNIPERS ELUDE TRAP ON ROOFTOP OF HOTEL
> *States-Item* (New Orleans), Monday, January 8, 1973a
> NO TRACE OF SNIPER FOUND AFTER POLICE COMB HOTEL

and

Introduction

HUNT FOR DEADLY SNIPER CONTINUES
   The Times-Picayune (New Orleans), Tuesday Morning, January 9, 1973a, b
MAYOR FEARS 'SNIPER 2' WILL REMAIN MYSTERY
   The States-Item, Thursday, January 11, 1973

In time the police officially determined was that there had ("probably") been only one sniper, Mark Essex, but some participants in the event still continue to maintain the existence of a second sniper.

How is evidence *actually* used to construct an Other when the very existence of that Other is problematic? And how is it used to unconstitute that Other? I seek answers in the practices employed in the Case of the New Orleans Sniper.

THE DATA

The data is drawn primarily from contemporary reports in two New Orleans newspapers, *The Times-Picayune* (T-P) and the *States-Item* (S-I), and from the 889-page August 31, 1973 New Orleans Police Department Report (PR)[9]. I have generally relied on newspaper reports at the time of the event for descriptions of the constitution of the second sniper and on the Police Report for descriptions of the unconstitution of that second sniper. Additional data is from videotapes of CBS, ABC, and NBC television news at the time of the event; written summaries from Vanderbilt University Television News Archive; and my own memories of hearing and reading about the event as it unfolded. I have used Peter Hernon's *A Terrible Thunder: The Story of the New Orleans Sniper* (1978/2001) to supplement or clarify some points, especially those related to information available well after the event.

The primary materials upon which I have drawn—newspaper and police reports—are not offered as objective and factual, for, as with all documentary sources, they are influenced by the authors' projects and audiences. "Newsworthy" stories and "justifiable" police work certainly frame these materials. Both, however, rely upon and provide versions of common-sense accounts of the doings of a problematic Other. Acknowledging the contexts within which they were created, these accounts nonetheless provide rich descriptions of ways that an Other can be conceptualized.

TIMELINE OF KEY EVENTS

These are events deemed relevant by 1/10/73 but not necessarily seen as linked as the event was unfolding. The times given follow the Police Report. The discussion of unconstituting the Other and the Appendix offer witnesses' statements that set some of the events at an earlier time.

SUNDAY, 12/31/72 10:55 p.m.	Killing at Central Lockup of Police Cadet Alfred Harrell and wounding of Lieutenant Horace Perez
Approximately 11:00 p.m.	Patrolman Edwin S. Hosli Sr. shot at Burkart Manufacturing Company (died almost two months later)
SUNDAY, 1/7/73 Approximately 10:30 a.m.	Shooting of grocer Joseph Perniciaro at his grocery store
Shortly after 10:30 a.m.	Marvin Albert's car stolen
10:45 a.m.	First sightings of sniper inside hotel; first fire noticed on 18th floor
10:52 a.m.	First fire alarm
11:00 a.m.	First shots fired
10:57 a.m.–12:10 p.m.	Sniper shootings from patio (11:02 firefighter shot)
12:10 p.m.	Sniper fired through door into 4th floor garage
12:18 p.m.–12:34 p.m.	Sniper shots from 16th floor
12:55 p.m.	Fires set on 17th floor
1:07 p.m.	Police Chief Sirgo shot in 17th–18th floor stairwell
1:12 p.m.	Sniper sighted on hotel roof
Approximately 8:50 p.m.	MARK ESSEX KILLED
MONDAY, 1/8/73 5:00 a.m.	4 policemen in stairwell and 2 in helicopter wounded by gunfire (later attributed to police)
About 11:30 a.m.	A rash of reports of gunfire and of an additional sniper or snipers and suspicious persons seen at several locations; bomb threats
1:45–2:00 p.m.	Assault on rooftop, 3 policemen wounded (later attributed to police ricochets)
1/8/73, 3:30 p.m.	Search of air conditioning units

SUNDAY DEATHS: 6 (3 New Orleans policemen, a motel assistant manager, a doctor and his wife); a 7th (hotel general manager) died later.
SUNDAY WOUNDINGS: 10

NOTES

1. I have cited various materials from Husserl's Second, Third, and Fifth Meditations (in *Cartesian Meditations*). I note from which Meditation I have drawn, adding "Cartesian," although in Husserl's text they are simply titled "First Meditation," etc.
2. Much to my surprise, I discovered that Husserl, in *Experience and Judgment*, uses just such a mannequin example (1973: 92).
3. For further discussion and other examples of "problematic Others," see Waksler, "Analogues of Ourselves: Who Counts as an Other?" (2005).
4. In what follows, citations are primarily from *Cartesian Meditations* since that work was most directly relevant, but other works of Husserl (cited in the Bibliography) undergird my analysis. I have also drawn on the Husserl-inspired work of Maxine Sheets-Johnstone.
5. Information in brackets [ ] refers to Carr's emendation of Husserl's statements in his English translation.
6. Certainly there have been other snipers in New Orleans, but "The" New Orleans Sniper is still heard as referring to this event.
7. Some newspaper reports refer to the Howard Johnson's Motor Lodge or Motor Hotel; following the New Orleans Police Department report, I have used "Motel" throughout (or simply Howard Johnson's) but have maintained other usages as they appear in quotations from the data. The same place is being designated.
8. Although there were some reports of a third and even fourth sniper, the search focused primarily on a second sniper, who is the focus of my consideration.
9. The Report includes the following topics: time sequence outline, narrative of the event, descriptions of scenes, physical evidence, other investigations, exhibits, and complete texts of original statements and interviews of police officers, firemen, Howard Johnson's guests and employees, and other witnesses. I reviewed 132 interviews with police officers related to all the linked events. Interviews with police officers regarding the specific event at Howard Johnson's were conducted from January 9 through February 2 on an almost daily basis. (No interviews were dated 1/13, 1/14, 1/21, 1/28, and 1/29, and 2/1.) Interviews were also provided for 9 firefighters, 42 hotel guests, 14 hotel employees, and 32 other witnesses.

CHAPTER 2.
CONSTITUTING THE OTHER: THE CONTEXT

What is an Other made of? Out of what elements in any specific situation can an Other be constituted? Based on my analysis of data concerning the New Orleans Sniper, I offer the following general claims: Prior assumptions and expectations create a space for the Other. Immediate concerns and needs outline that space. The space thus created is filled in with common-sense ideas about what an Other is and is not capable of and with sights, sounds, and indications of turn-taking. These are linked by common-sense theories and speculation, all to some extent constrained by the outline. New or reformulated assumptions and evidence, however, can change the meaning of the constituent elements or change the very outline itself. When expectations change, when the *existence* of an Other is denied, the same evidence can, though with varying degrees of difficulty, be reinterpreted to support the *nonexistence* of that Other. In that process, both the evidence and those who provide it can come in for reassessment and reevaluation.

The Case of the New Orleans Sniper serves as both a source of these claims and their illustration. In what follows I document the use of these ideas in constituting the New Orleans (second) sniper. The central question is: How did a second sniper come to be constituted, to continue to be constituted after the death of the first sniper, Mark Essex, and in time come to be unconstituted?

THE IMMEDIATE CONTEXT FOR ASSUMPTIONS[1]

Construction of an Other takes place within a social framework in which claims of an Other's existence are plausible and may be either confirmed or denied either by others present at the time or retrospectively. To understand the evidence used to support the existence of another (second) sniper, I begin with the proximate events, cited in newspaper articles at the time, in the context of which that evidence was used. Of immediate relevance was that on New Year's Eve, 12/31/72, a week before the Howard Johnson's Motel sniping, a police cadet was killed at Central Lockup and a police lieutenant was wounded. Shortly thereafter, a patrolman was shot at the Burkart Manufacturing Company. No assailant was identified and the police were unsure whether there were one or more assailants.

Between these shootings and the first fire set at the Howard Johnson's Motel on 1/7/73, police were searching for an assailant or assailants and following up leads. At the same time, police were investigating a number of reports of activities that may or may not have been related (indeed may or may not have been substantiated): shots fired, sightings of snipers, stolen cars, and suspicious fires. It was unclear which events were linked, which independent, and how many people were involved, but the stage was set for the plausible assumption that, if some or all of these events were linked, more than one person could be involved in the event that unfolded at the Howard Johnson's Motel on Sunday morning, 1/7/73.

As the sniping began on that morning, of particular immediate contextual significance in understanding the postulation of more than one sniper are the turmoil, conflicting reports, poor visibility (from the fires set and the light rain falling), the necessity for and urgency of acting, and the life and death significance of actions taken. Newspaper excerpts from a later police report state,

> The number and location of fires on several levels of the motel, the killing committed on different levels, the snipings from various levels, all in combination were sufficient to create a reasonable belief that there was more than one person involved in the acts of killings and arson on Jan. 7, 1973. . . .Following Mark Essex's slaying, it was determined that due caution be exercised to insure that further unnecessary killings be prevented (quoted in T-P, 2/20/73, and cited above).

Also contributing to the confusion were the arrival on the scene of a number of police from other departments, at times unknown to and unrecognized by the central command; limited communications resources; and a number of private citizens armed and eager to help. Hernon describes police as being "out of touch with the command post. . . ." (1978/2001: 187). Detective Roland Forman, for example, arriving on the scene, stated, "We waited at the Command Post [in the hotel] for instructions as to where we should go, and after receiving none, we started looking for an area where we could view the top of the building" (PR: 408). Other police officers similarly acted on their own. Final estimates of police on the scene run as high as 700.

Further confusing the situation, "About midday [Monday, 1/8/73, the day after Essex's death], police began to be plagued by a rash of reports of shootings, new snipers and bomb scares in various parts of the city" (S-I, 1/8/73a). Hernon offers details.

> By ten o'clock [Monday]. . .Dispatchers received incoherent reports that snipers were firing from rooftops in other parts of the city; a woman was said to have been wounded in the head; blacks with rifles were allegedly seen darting down alleys, firing as they ran; and a black couple driving an expensive car had reportedly just purchased a large quantity of ammunition. One sighting seemed to trigger three

more, and as each call was checked out and proven erroneous, others poured into the command post (Hernon, 1978/2001: 241).

After Essex's death on Sunday evening, given the danger presented by a second sniper, caution recommended that the police as well as the public adopt minimal standards for assuming that such a one existed. Thus,

> A 50-square-block area in the vicinity of the hotel in the central business district was declared off-limits Monday to vehicular and pedestrian traffic. Authorities wanted no one endangered by stray bullets while the intensive search was being made by scores of policemen for the source of sniper fire (S-I, 1/9/73a).

At least three people who said they saw a sniper were interviewed after Essex's death and asked newspaper reporters for anonymity, suggesting that they were afraid of a second sniper.

> Asked if he [Beamish], a hotel guest] could describe the gunman, he said, 'Yes, I could, but discretion is the better part of valor because the man they shot (on the roof of the Howard Johnson Hotel here Sunday) is not the same man who shot me'. . . .[H]e was wary of receiving any publicity because he was afraid the sniper might return to slay him (S-I, 1/10/73, byline Eric Newhouse, AP).

Police who were wounded after Essex's death and police who were shooting at what they thought was a second sniper may have had particular reason for wanting there to be a second sniper. Police Officer O'Sullivan, for example, was said to be "convinced he was shot by a sniper. The hole in his ear now held together by stitches is proof enough for him, he said" (S-I, 1/9/73, byline Angus Lind). If there was no second sniper, it might turn out that police officers had been shooting at one another, a conclusion that there was some reluctance to draw.

The failure to either identify or reject the existence of a second sniper was seen to have particular implications for race relations.

> [B]lack leaders fume over the delay of city officials to say once and for all that Essex was a loner without help. . . .That delay encourages white apprehensions that one or two black revolutionary triggermen are still at large (Robert Novak, national columnist, quoted in S-I, 2/15/73, byline Allan Katz).

If a second sniper existed, clearly police and the public were in danger. If, however, it was determined that there had been only one sniper all along, actions after Essex's death, especially those of the police, could be open to criticism if not ridicule. Nonetheless, "[New Orleans Police Superintendent] Giarrusso said there was too much evidence of a second sniper to abandon the idea completely" (S-I, 1/10/73b).

Preliminary features of the situation thus facilitated the postulation of a second sniper: the ambiguity of events during the previous week; the confusion at the scene; and the serious consequences if there were a second sniper. Police Supt. Clarence B. Giarrusso said, "You have to realize that in the thick of things I had some judgment decisions to make" (T-P, 1/10/73, byline Emile LaFourcade). Given the importance of determining whether or not there was a second sniper, what evidence did the police and others use at the time to come to the "reasonable" belief or "best" or "wisest" guess that a second sniper indeed existed?

THE POWER OF FIRST ASSUMPTIONS

As the sniping began at the Howard Johnson's Motel, the initial *assumption* that there was more than one sniper served to frame and legitimate evidence for the *existence* of more than one sniper[2] and foreclosed, for some time and for many of those involved, attribution of the acts to a single person. First reports were of particular significance. NBC-TV reported as the event was under way, "It is believed that one sniper may have held as many as a dozen hostages while a second man ran from floor to floor firing at police from different vantage points" (1/7/73, 5:30 p.m.).[3]

Police reporting to the scene had been informed of the event in a variety of ways. Some were phoned by Police Office John April, New Orleans Criminal Investigation Division, though how he described the situation at Howard Johnson's is not mentioned. A number heard the news on public radio, so those reports were particularly consequential in establishing first assumptions. One heard of the event through his wife who heard it from another wife (PR: 553); a firefighter heard it from his mother (PR: 627). Certainly some police arrived on the scene "knowing" that there was more than one sniper.

Early newspaper reports described "a sniper or snipers," though some settled on the more ambiguous "sniping." Two police officers arriving on the scene "heard the story: An uncertain number of militants had taken over the Howard Johnson's, killed a honeymooning couple and a hotel official, started fires on several floors and then began pouring shots on arriving firemen and police" (T-P, 1/11/87, byline Ronnie Virgets). Against this background, standards of evidence for a second sniper may have been lower than if the initial assumption had been of *one* sniper.

The death of Mark Essex did not foreclose the possible existence of a second sniper.

> The theory of two or more snipers was based on evidence which included reports of gunfire coming from the roof and the wounding of three policemen in a stairwell between the 18th floor and the roof, long after the first sniper had been slain (S-I, 1/9/73b).

Given the initial assumption and supporting evidence for the existence of a second sniper, until the time that police stormed the bunker on the hotel roof on

Monday, 1/8 and found it empty, there seemed little reason to seriously question the existence of a second sniper.[4] After the failure to find that second sniper on the roof or later in the air conditioning ducts, the non-existence of a second sniper took on more plausibility, though not certainty, and especially not for those whose own experiences convinced them otherwise.

Thus one element in support of evidence for an Other is the expectation that there *is* an Other. The expectation creates a space within which to constitute that Other. Such an expectation can be supported both by common-sense knowledge of what is possible for one person to do as well as by the direct evidence of one's senses.

NOTES

1. Previous fires set in New Orleans, police concern about black militant groups locally and nationally, and other factors may well have provided a general background for the assumptions made in this case. The broader historical context for the assumptions, despite its general relevance, is beyond the scope of this project.

2. The power of initial assumptions is starkly exemplified by the Charles "Chuck" Stuart case (10/23/89, Boston, MA). Videotape as he was brought into the emergency ward showed police and medical personnel saying that he had been shot twice. The initial assumption that Stuart was shot not once but twice lent credence, if credence was even needed, to his claim that he had been shot by someone else rather than, as later emerged, by himself (and shot only once). Here the assumption seemed to be that nobody would (or could?) shoot himself twice.

3. Later information suggests that those taken to be hostages—hotel guests and a hotel maid seen on the patio—were simply present along with the sniper rather than hostages, although the sniper did shoot one of them.

4. One police officer interviewed on television maintained at the time of the event that there was only one sniper, but his conviction does not seem to have been widely shared at first.

CHAPTER 3.
CONSTITUTING THE OTHER:
THE EVIDENCE

> It is clear that truth or the true actuality of objects is to be obtained only from *evidence*, and that it is evidence alone by virtue of which an *"actually" existing*, true, rightly accepted object of whatever form or kind *has sense for us*—and with all the determinations that for us belong to it under the title of its true nature (Husserl, Third Cartesian Meditation, 1960: 60, emphasis in original).

Crucial here is the phrase "has sense for us." The existence of a "second sniper" initially seemed to make "more sense" than the existence of only one sniper and thus guided the search for evidence. Evidence, however, conflicted and its meaning and significance changed over time. New evidence was offered, old evidence reevaluated. Some of what had been taken to be evidence was retrospectively rejected or reformulated. Evidence is thus not static but itself socially constructed.

The following accounts, offered in the days after Essex's death and the failure to find a second sniper, describe the ambiguous nature of the available evidence.

> Were there one, two, or three snipers? The people who are having the most trouble making up their minds and are most eager to wait until all the evidence is sorted out tend to be those who were there. All the signs pointed to more than one gunman until the final assault on the rooftop that came up empty-handed. People who have been in combat tell me that one sniper who was very cool and very good at his business, could have done everything—set the fires, moved from area to area of the hotel quickly, fired with great accuracy on police and firemen, battled with the helicopter.
>
> But, how then do we explain the voices heard on the rooftop after Mark Essex was killed? Or, the gunshots that seemed to come from the rooftop? The theory about the sniper slipping through the police sounds okay until you examine it. It would take a very cool operator indeed to walk past police—which he would have had to

> do—after having been in a combat situation for at least 10 hours or more (S-I, 1/12/73, byline Allan Katz).

> [Police Superintendent. Clarence B.] Giarrusso acknowledged yesterday that he no longer is "certain" that more than one sniper was in the hotel, but he did not dismiss the theory.... The superintendent said at the same time there is equally strong evidence to indicate there was more than one sniper as there is to support the claim of only one sniper (S-I, 1/10/73a, byline Lanny Thomas).

The evidence used to constitute an Other, the "second sniper," was a pastiche of everyday life assumptions: the initial assumption that there simply *was* (or had to be) more than one sniper; assumptions about what one person is capable and incapable of doing; assumptions about the meaning of sights, sounds, and leavings (what was left behind); and speculation, including the postulation of a conspiracy, to blend the evidence into a coherent whole. Husserl writes,

> Daily practical living is naïve. It is immersion in the already-given world, whether it be experiencing, or thinking, or valuing, or acting. Meanwhile all those productive intentional functions of experiencing, because of which physical things are simply there, go on anonymously. The experiencer knows nothing about them, and likewise nothing about his productive thinking. The numbers, the predicative complexes of affairs, the goods, the ends, the works, present themselves because of the hidden performances; they are built up, member by member; they alone are regarded (Fifth Cartesian Meditation, 1960: 152–3).

What were the constituents of these hidden performances by which a second sniper, an Other, was constituted? The first, and at the time especially compelling, evidence for more than one sniper was the idea that one person could not have done all that was done.

WHAT ONE PERSON IS CAPABLE OF DOING: MARK ESSEX (THE "FIRST" SNIPER)

> [W]hat motivates my experience of the other immediately and directly as "someone else" is the experience of an animate form similar to my own: formal similarities motivate the apperceptive transfer of sense. On the basis of these formal similarities, I apprehend the other in ways coincident with my sphere of ownness: the other too has fields of sensation; the other too governs spontaneously and freely in its own movement; the other too has a repertoire of I cans; the other too is reflexively related to itself as an object of sense; the other too is a psychophysical unity. In a word, the other too is a kinetic/tactile-kinesthetic body (Sheets-Johnstone, 1999: 100–1).

Others are subject to common-sense rules including the general rule of "acting like a person" (specifically, acting like *one* person). Throughout initial reports, common-sense claims are made about what one person (sniper or not) is capable of accomplishing. If more is done than one person can do, it follows that there must be at least a second person. Thus, "Many are still wondering how one sniper could account for so many fires, six deaths, innumerable woundings and injuries" (S-I, 1/9/73, byline Angus Lind).

What exactly, and how much, can one *ordinary*[1] person do? In part this question reflects ideas about physical possibilities. Persons are subject to physical laws, *however those laws are formulated.* One ordinary person, for example, is not routinely expected to be in two places at once—and claims of being so can turn out to be somewhat problematic. There was, for example,

> [a] report that a neighbor [of Essex], Edwin L. Wilson, 76, said he was given a lift to church by Essex in a dark blue car at 11:45 a.m. last Sunday [1/7/73]. Given the assumption that it is impossible to be in two places at once, this report would place Essex away from the hotel at the time the fires and shootings are believed to have begun (S-I, 1/15/73, byline John Kifner, *New York Times*).

Essex's death and identification as *a* sniper if not *the* sniper would seem to lead to one of two explanations for Wilson's claim: that Wilson was mistaken about who gave him a ride (or, perhaps, when) or that there was indeed a second sniper.[2]

The following accounts offered evidence that one person could not do what was done:

> According to police, the snipers went from room to room in the hotel, beginning about 11 a.m., setting fires. Then, as police and firemen responded to each new fire, the snipers shot at them. At the same time, the snipers kept up withering fire at Duncan Plaza in the Civic Center, hitting several policemen (S-I, 1/8/73a).

> [Fire Supt. Louis San Salvador said] he 'can't believe we've caught all the gunmen. . . . [He] said his men found fires in the 8th, 9th, 15th, 16 and 17th floors of the hotel, in the front and the back. . . .'There is at least one more [sniper] and he just walked away from it,' he said. . . . For one man to move around like that setting fires and shooting—it would be very, very hard to do' (S-I, 1/16/73a).

> [John Tobin, hotel guest, said] 'The first smoke we saw was coming from the 18th floor. Then it seemed like as soon as the sniper stepped back in, then the fire broke out on the eighth floor. We'd hear someone shoot, then we'd hear return fire (the police), then we'd see a new fire break out some place. It don't seem to me possible that one man could have done it all. It seemed like he'd shoot and then a new fire would break out several doors away. Seemed like each time there was a new shooting, a new fire would break out,' Tobin said. 'I could

see both the front of the building and the back of the building. He'd fire once from the front of the building and then maybe fire would break out in the back of the building. It didn't seem possible that one man could run that fast and start those fires' (T-P 1/12/73, byline John McMillan).

A determination of what one *ordinary* person is capable of doing leads to the issue of what one *extraordinary* person might accomplish. Was the sniper (or, initially, snipers) very smart, very skilled, very well organized, or simply very lucky? Was the event carefully planned or did it just unfold? Initial reports spoke of expertise. Reporter Dempsey referred to the snipers' "deadly accuracy" (S-I 1/8/73, byline Jack Dempsey). Carolyn Strecker, hotel guest, said, "The guy was really a good shot" (S-I, 1/10/73a). Two snipers were said to be "well armed and well entrenched" (ABC-TV, 1/8/73, 5:01, 5:15 p.m.). "Police. . .say the snipers are skillful in the use of firearms, had a good plan which did not seem to envision an escape from the motel and embarked on their mission well prepared for most eventualities" (S-I, 1/8/73a). Later newspaper reports, however, suggest less expertise.

> 'The arson was not planned. The sniper went from room to room igniting whatever he could, and if the object didn't catch fire, then he would go on to something else. Boxes of matches were found everywhere,' [Assistant Fire Supt. William] McCrossen said (T-P, 1/12/73, byline Maren Rudolph).

> His [Essex's] conduct at the hotel, according to the [status] report [by the New Orleans Police Department], convinced the police that he did not know the floor plan. For example, he had to ask hotel employees how to get from the parking garage, where he left the stolen auto, into the hotel (S-I, 2/20/73, byline Allan Katz).

The skill of the sniper(s) would seem to be especially significant for police, especially if there was only one sniper. If the attack was well planned, the participant(s) skilled, then the police response can be seen as fitting. If, however, a lone and not particularly skilled sniper "held 500 police officers and virtually all of New Orleans at bay" (ABC-TV, 1/8/73, 5:01, 5:16 p.m.), the police might appear both inefficient and duped.

Common-sense ideas about human capabilities thus played a part in postulating a second sniper. Once a determination was made that one person, either ordinary or even extraordinary, was not capable of doing what was done, the postulation of a second person was taken to be the most plausible alternative. Later, once the idea of only one sniper became plausible, the question changed to: *how* could one person accomplish what was accomplished? Even later the question was reformulated: how much of what was done was done by the sniper and how much done by police or others (nonsnipers)? In the midst of the event, however, a wide range of actions was attributed in such a way that one person would have been incapable of carrying out all of them.

SIGNS OF AN OTHER

A number of features of an Other can be derived from an examination of the process whereby a second sniper was initially postulated: Others are taken to be seeable, capable of sound and thus hearable, and capable of movement and action. Sights, sounds, and indications of action can thereby "stand for" an Other. Reciprocity, i.e., turn-taking, can serve as especially compelling evidence. Others can leave traces—objects and other tangible "artifacts." Speculation, including here conspiracy theories, can be used to fill in the emerging picture. The existence of a given Other may, nonetheless, remain relative and tentative. In what follows I detail how certain features of Others were used to constitute a specific Other (a second sniper)–the very same features that were later used to unconstitute that Other.

Others Are Seeable

Sightings of *two* different snipers were initially accepted as clear evidence of their existence. Such sightings were taken to be expected, given the context and initial assumptions, but sightings served as compelling evidence in themselves.

> [H]armonious appresentations are a matter not of behavior as such but of movement. Certain spatio-temporal-energic dynamics of movement link us harmoniously together and ground our continuing sense of the other as 'someone else' (Sheets-Johnstone, 1999: 102).

It is just this movement (or indicators of it) that served as evidence of a second sniper.

Prior to Essex's death, the sighting of a single person at different times and by different witnesses raised the issue of whether these sightings were of the same or a different person.[3] Eyewitnesses are said to be unreliable (when eyewitnesses agree, are they thereby reliable?), but how great must the discrepancies be before the postulation of two distinct people is warranted? Differences in skin color, gender, and the presence/absence of a goatee may be more definitive than differences in size and clothing.

Essex was described in the Police Report as a Negro male, 5'7", 141 lbs., age 23. His body on the roof of the Howard Johnson's was

> attired in a green long sleeved shirt, black pullover short sleeved shirt, brown leather belt, green army fatigue pants with large side pockets and black military combat boots. Next to the body was a .44 caliber magnum rifle (PR: 167).

Some witness accounts were close enough to this description to support the claim that they were indeed of Essex, given an assumption of some minor eyewitness unreliability. After Essex's death, witnesses were shown his photograph and some identified him as the person they had seen.

There were, however, reports of a person sighted before Essex's death who was described as significantly different from Essex and taken to be a second sniper. Some offered descriptions difficult or impossible to reconcile with Essex's appearance and taken as evidence of a second sniper.

> Many of the early descriptions of the sniper, or snipers, told of a tall, lanky, light-skinned Negro with a goatee (S-I, 1/15/73, byline John Kifner, *New York Times*).

Others who offered descriptions similar to Essex's were shown his photograph and denied that he was the person they saw.

> 'The man they shot on the roof is not the same man who shot me,' one of Sunday's sniping victims said here Tuesday. 'The man who shot me had on a light tan jacket and brown slacks,' said Robert Beamish. . . .Could one gunman have changed clothes? Police are unsure. . . .[Beamish said,] 'He was slender and fairly light colored. . . and about the same height I am, 5 foot-8". . . .For about three and one-half hours, Beamish played possum in the pool, watching the sniper pop in and out of various hotel rooms and listening to the shooting and the gunfire (T-P, 1/10/73, byline Eric Newhouse, AP).[4]

Some witnesses (hotel employees and guests) had face-to-face interactions with a sniper. Such witnesses might be taken to be particularly reliable, given their direct contact. Although some identified Essex from photos, others could not identify any photo and yet others identified someone other than Essex. That witnesses interacted with *some* Other is not at issue; they all directly grasped an Other as an Other. The issue is whether they "grasped" the same or different people.

A number of sightings by hotel maids included interactions of varying length with the presumed sniper or snipers. Carolyn Ardis, who saw a person through a small window in the 8th floor stairwell door, said, "[H]e just kept asking me if I would open the door for him, and I kept telling him no" (PR: 796). Hazel Thomas, looking through the same stairwell door, said,

> The negro male asked me to open the door for him and said that he knew somebody on the 18th floor, and that somebody had shown him the way in. I told him that I couldn't open the door for him because it was against motel rules. While I was talking to him, Carolyn [Ardis], who was working on the floor with me, came to the door. He then asked us if we were soul sisters. We told him we were and that's when he said, 'One for all and two for one' (PR: 828).

Annie McCoy said,

> I saw a negro male through the small window in the door [of the 9th floor stairwell], and he was begging me to open the door. Then I told him I couldn't open the door, I had to go get the inspector. And he asked me if he could get in on the upper floor, and I told him I didn't know. He went up the steps and then I heard three shots. . .(PR: 822).

Delores Arnold said, "He walked towards us [along the 18th floor corridor] and stopped and told us that he wasn't going to hurt us, and we went back into the [hotel] room" (PR: 799). Carrie Mae Clemmons, describing a sniper's entrance from the 11th floor stairwell, said, "He just came walking through with his head down, in a big hurry" (PR: 803). He said, "I'm going to keep killing all the white people." To the interviewer's question, "He said that to you?" she replied, "He was just saying it. He didn't say it to me, he said it when he entered the hall door" (PR: 804). And he said, "You all go ahead, I ain't killing you black people" (PR: 805). Beatrice Greenhouse stated, "When he came out in the hall [on the 11th floor], the man told me that this was a revolution and that he was only shooting whites" (PR: 815). Later, when she was on the 8th floor patio, "I saw the negro male with the gun in a crouched position. I asked the negro male where I could go, and he told me which way to go" (PR: 815).

Despite the hotel maids' direct contract, they did not agree on the description of the person they saw. Shown photos, some identified Essex, others were not sure, some identified photos of someone else, yet others said that they did not know, and at least one denied vehemently that Essex was the person seen. (Further details of the maids' descriptions are provided in Chapter 4, "Others are Seeable: Retrospective Sightings" and the Appendix.)

A hotel guest also reported interacting with a sniper on the 8th floor patio. Timothy Michael Carew said he saw an armed black male with a medium afro who was crouched behind a planter on the patio:

> I saw the woman [Beatrice Greenhouse, hotel maid] on the ledge screaming for help and I saw the fire. On the way back in the room, I spotted the guy behind the bushes with the gun. The guy with the gun said to the lady on the ledge, 'The revolution is here,' then he pointed the gun at me and I went back inside. . . .We stayed in the room for a few minutes until the smoke was too much, then I opened the door to the patio and asked the man with the gun if we could come out. The man told me yes. We went over to the ledge by the lady, and we stood there for about ten minutes, so the firemen could see us. . .(PR: 635).

Carew identified one of nine photos but could not say positively and the Police Report does not indicate whose photo (#48378) he identified.

The evidence of those who had face-to-face contact with the sniper would seem to be of particular importance. Those who identified a photo of Essex could, at least in retrospect, be seen as reliable; those who could not and those who identified photos other than Essex's provide evidence for a second sniper–unless those identifications can be otherwise explained.

Prior to Essex's death, the sighting of two (or even three) possible snipers *together* served as evidence for the existence of more than one sniper. Joseph M. Rault Jr., owner of the Rault Center, "said that one of his employees saw two other people—a man and a woman—with the sniper. The woman was dressed in a uniform, he said" (T-P, 2/16/73, byline Paul Atkinson).

> A prominent New Orleans businessman has told Police Supt. Clarence B. Giarrusso that he saw two persons—one with a handgun—on the 17th floor balcony of the Downtown Howard Johnson's Motor Hotel the day of the sniper tragedy. . . .The man, who asked that he remain unidentified, said he believes one of the persons was light skinned and may have been white. . . .The man said he and a friend from Georgia saw two persons on the balcony from his office on Perdido Street. . . .He described the gunman as light-skinned, tall and heavy, and clad in khaki clothes. Moments later, the businessman said, a second person joined the gunman on the balcony. . . .The second man was smaller and darker, and was not armed. . . .He said three other rooms started blazing shortly after the pair left the balcony (S-I, 1/19/73, byline Jack Dempsey).

> [Jefferson Parish sheriff's Deputy David Munch] said yesterday that a sniper accompanied by a woman fired at him from the eighth floor patio of the hotel. Munch said he saw a black man with a woman shortly after 11:00 a.m. Sunday. . . .He said he spotted the woman about an hour later, when he was on the street. She was looking over the balcony[5] (S-I, 1/12/73a).

> Munch said his partner, Dep. Victor Hurregi, saw her, too. He said she was wearing a light brown overcoat. He added, 'This woman could have been a man. It could have been a stud with long hair, you can't tell these days. But it looked like, just looked like a woman.' He said the man was wearing a black shirt and 'in my opinion he had a goatee' (T-P, 1/12/73, byline John McMillan).

> Another person, who asked that his name not be used 'because he's (the second sniper) still on the loose,' said he saw two persons together on the eighth floor of the hotel between 11 a.m. and noon. That was after he saw one sniper, whom he said was not the slain Mark Essex, alone. . . .He described the man as being about 5-feet, 9-inches tall with light skin and a 'bush' haircut. He said he was wearing dark pants and a grey jacket, and had a 'big belt' around his waist. After being shot at, the eyewitness said he went down to the street and got some policemen who he took to the eighth floor of the Rault Center. They looked out of a window, he said, and saw the light-skinned man emerge from the sliding glass doors of a room near the Gravier-Rampart corner of the hotel and hide in the bushes on the

pool deck. He said the sniper had his rifle in his right hand. Then the sniper motioned with his left hand for his companion to remain in the hotel room 'The one in the room was short and skinny and had dark skin,' he said. 'He was the one who got killed' (T-P, 1/12/73, byline John McMillan).

After Essex's death, the sighting of a person taken to be a sniper takes on a very different kind of significance. A helicopter on loan from the Marine Corps continued to fly over the hotel, firing at the roof. (During the entire event the helicopter with armed patrolmen would make 48 passes over the hotel and fire hundreds of shots [Hernon, 1978: 200].) Marine Lieutenant Colonel Charles H. Pitman was quoted as saying, "We always thought there were at least three snipers, and that they had automatic weapons" (in Hernon, 1978/2001: 199; see also 217–8, 230–3). Sunday night about 11:30 p.m. one of the helicopter crew said,

> 'We saw him (the second sniper). He was curled around a drain pipe [a thick standpipe in the blockhouse], using it for a shield and we could not get our fire at him from our angle. We took fire from him' (S-I, 1/9/73, byline Allan Katz).

Police radio reports concurred with the presence of a second sniper.

> [Monday, after 1:00 a.m.] the police said a sniper had crawled across the roof and was firing at police from a ledge and was a difficult target because he was moving frequently. . . .Police on the roof of the Supreme Court Building in Duncan Plaza said on the radio they could see the sniper. . . .From the radio came such comments as, 'You're about two feet above him. Now you're on him. He's moving, he's moving. Your ricochets are missing him by inches' (S-I, 1/9/73, byline Allan Katz).

Shortly before dawn on Monday, four officers were wounded:

> [T]he sniper emerged briefly from the roof's concrete bunker. 'He popped at us, and we popped back,' said [Police Officer] O'Sullivan . . . .The sniper was about 20 feet from the three officers, he said. . . .He said the sniper apparently knew police were in the stairwell because he opened the door only part of the way and began to shoot (S-I, 1/8/73, byline Angus Lind).

About 2:00 Monday afternoon, with live television coverage, police stormed the roof and, to the clear surprise of those involved, no second sniper was discovered. Police department detective Guy LeBlanc, wounded at the bunker assault on Monday afternoon, said,

> We fired on the door [of the bunker], then some of us were wounded. I don't know whether we were hit from fire from inside or outside the enclosure. I thought it was from inside (T-P, 1/9/73, byline Joan Treadway).

After no second sniper was found on the roof, three air conditioning units on the roof and air conditioning ducts in the hotel were searched. "[I]t was reported that an officer saw a black male 'eyeball to eyeball' hiding in a duct [but] "[e]ven after ripping apart air conditioning units"] nothing was uncovered" (S-I, 1/9/73, byline Angus Lind). And finally, Monday afternoon,

> after the 'second sniper' could not be found, it was reported widely a black man had been seen on Melpomene Street discarding a police jacket and running away. All the reports turned out to be false (S-I, 1/9/73, byline Allan Katz).

Those who were convinced that Essex was the person they saw neither refuted nor confirmed the existence of a second sniper. But what of those who were convinced that they saw another person with Essex or saw a second sniper, someone who "couldn't" be Essex?

> Honesty is not all, by any means, that is necessary to being believed. It is impossible to convey a conviction of anything. All you can do is to convey a conviction that you are convinced. Of course, what satisfied you might satisfy another; but, till you can present him with the sources of your conviction, you cannot present him with the conviction—and perhaps not even then (Macdonald, 1869: 135).

Either these sightings of a second sniper confirmed the existence of an Other or the claims themselves were open to refutation, either at the time or later, either by the claimant or by others. In the process of refutation by others, claimants might find themselves—their perceptions, their reasoning, their reliability, their convictions, the very evidence of their senses—challenged, denigrated, rejected. Nonetheless, seeing a second sniper, either with Essex, different from Essex, or after Essex's death, was taken initially as confirmation of the existence of an Other.

The statement that "Others are seeable," despite its apparent straightforwardness, turns out to gloss a complex set of processes. *Seeing* a second sniper, either with Essex, different from Essex, or after Essex's death, was taken initially as self-evident confirmation of the existence of an Other—certain enough that police fired their weapons at that Other. Later the self-evidentiary quality of sightings came in for questioning, reassessment, and alternative explanation.

Others and Their Actions Are Hearable

Sounds—both gunfire and voices—supplemented sightings and also served as evidence in their own right of a second sniper. Both gunfire and voices can be ambiguous and require interpretive work. Gunshots do not disclose *who* is doing the shooting, a point that became relevant in the aftermath of the event when it was determined that on some occasions police might have been shooting at one another. Ricochets and echoes can confuse comprehension of the direction from which shots are coming. Voices too can be problematic, for inferences are required to determine *who* is speaking and *to whom*. Some attribution of voices to a sniper rested on common-sense ideas of what kinds of thing a sniper would be likely to say and nonsnipers unlikely to say.

Prior to Essex's death, gunfire was reported as coming from more than one direction at a time, more frequently than one person was thought capable of firing, and from different kinds of firearms. "Gunfire seemed to be going off all over, the reports echoing off the nearby higher buildings" (S-I, 1/15/73, byline John Kifner, *New York Times*). Certainly some of the gunfire could be attributed to police shooting at the sniper(s)—Hernon describes *undisciplined* police gunfire (1978: 136) and police "shooting wildly" (1978: 187). Some gunfire was so attributed at the time and even more in the aftermath. Nonetheless, at the time some gunfire was directly attributed to at least two snipers and served as evidence of a second sniper.

The simultaneity of the sounds of gunshots from different places (the "cannot be in two places at once" rule) and the postulation of different guns (perhaps a "one person/one gun" rule) supported the claim of a second sniper, as did gunfire in conjunction with sightings. Ed Frashier, hotel guest, said that he saw two men fighting in the hallway, then saw "a man's arm protruding from a door with a rifle in it," then heard gunfire from one of the rooms, then from more than one place on the roof. "I just feel there had to be more than one of them (snipers) because of the gunfire. . .at one point it seemed like it was coming from both sides and down to my left and above me." He said that "one rifle sounded like a cannon" (S-I, 1/9/73c). Another person who reported seeing two snipers prior to Essex's death said of the gunshots he heard, "The first two shots were loud . . . while the third was less noisy" (S-I, 1/10/73, byline Jack Dempsey). The linking of sounds and sightings served to reinforce each item of evidence taken separately, but sounds alone were deemed evidentiary.

Especially consequential for the postulation of a second sniper is that *after* Essex's death on Sunday, 1/7/73 at approximately 8:50 p.m., reports of sniper fire continued. "[New Orleans Police Superintendent] Giarrusso said that the pilot [of the helicopter] was certain the copter was shot after Essex was felled" (T-P, 1/10/73, byline Emile LaFourcade). At 1:00 a.m. Monday police stationed in a nearby building reported that "a sharp 'crack' as might be made by a handgun was heard repeatedly" (S-I, 1/9/73, byline Allan Katz). Monday afternoon, a report from the Charity Hospital emergency ward stated that "you could hear the steady not-too-distant *exchange* between the snipers and police in circling helicopters" (S-I, 1/8/73, byline Patsy Sims, emphasis added).

Hearing the voices of more than one person prior to Essex's death was also used as evidence of a second sniper. A police transmission, for example, reported, "We can hear at least two and possibly three persons yelling and cursing after the chopper went by!" (S-I 1/8/73, byline Jack Dempsey). *After* Essex's death, the hearing of a voice that could be attributed to a second (or even third) sniper lent further support to the existence of at least a second sniper.

> While I was in that position [19th floor stairwell], we were informed by police radio that one sniper was hit on the roof. As far as I can recall I feel that I heard *voices* coming from the roof, shouting 'Africa, Africa' (Police Officer Salvador Scalia, PR: 561–2, emphasis added).

> Several officers and newsmen who were located in the Rault Center and the Saratoga Building parking garage Sunday night maintained Tuesday they heard voices on the Howard Johnson's roof and that fire came from the rooftop after Essex was killed (T-P, 1/10/73, byline Emile LaFourcade).

> The police chief [Giarrusso]. . .said that many police on buildings near the roof heard shooting and talking after Essex was shot (T-P, 1/10/73, byline Emile LaFourcade).

Reporter[6] John McMillan described what he heard:

> At 1:40 a.m. Monday, hours after the sniper identified as Mark James Robert Essex, 23, was gunned down by police, I heard a shout, seemingly from atop the Downtown Howard Johnson Hotel. 'You honkie. . .pigs,' a voice shouted. It came about five minutes after a heavy barrage of gunfire from the Marine helicopter used in the attack. Then he yelled, 'Why don't you. . .come on the roof [and fight] like a black man.'

McMillan goes on to describe his conversation with three others with him.

> They too had heard the shouts, but weren't sure what he had said. They also had heard the obscenities. Later, after police had pounded the stairwell on the Gravier Street side of the hotel for one hour and 15 minutes to carve a hole in the reinforced concrete, we heard a shout: 'I'm still here you. . .' (T-P, 1/10/73, byline John McMillan).

Joe Manguno, a reporter for United Press International, offered detailed evidence of sounds *accompanied* by sightings. He described his observations after Essex's death.

> A figure of a face, a silhouette, protruded from the side of the cubicle with a rifle and there were two shots and two barrel flashes. . .and a voice very distinctly yelled 'Power to the people, power to the peo-

ple' and then an obscenity which I could hear echo. . . .I'm convinced I saw him (CBS-TV, 1/9/73, 5:42 p.m.).

'The helicopter continued firing for awhile, then went off to the left to the Civic Center,' Manguno said. 'Then a man stuck a rifle out of the concrete cubicle (on the Gravier St. side of the hotel roof), yelled 'power to the people' and fired twice at the helicopter. I commented on it with the policemen (on the 17th floor),' Manguno said. He said he didn't get the policemen's names because at the time everyone 'knew' there were two snipers, that it was inconceivable that anyone would think there was only one sniper. Even the police radio reported officers seeing two men fire at the helicopter following Essex's death (T-P, 1/12/73, byline John McMillan).

If Manguno and others did indeed hear these words, who other than a sniper would have occasion to say them? The words attributed to the "Other" are offered as the kind that a sniper who was black[7] might be thought to say and have reason to say and that Others would be far less likely to say and, in the context, have no reason to say. Hernon, however, offers evidence for an alternative explanation, of potential later use in unconstituting the second sniper: "Long into the night, police yelled insults from the Rault Center and other buildings as they tried to bait the gunmen into revealing their positions. . .'Power to the people, nigger'" (Hernon, 1978/2001: 227). Use of the word "nigger" here, for those who heard it, might well change the attribution of what was heard. Police might be more likely to use the word for purposes of baiting and a sniper who was black would seem to have little reason to use it in this context.

Here, as elsewhere, alternative explanations available at a later time could not, obviously, be of use in the throes of the event. What serves as the most plausible explanation at one time may be found wanting later. Some of the gunfire might be explained retrospectively as issuing from the police, but the voices and especially the words heard seem most plausibly assigned to a second sniper, at least unless the reports themselves are challenged or until other explanations become available and seem more plausible.

Turn-Taking (Reciprocity)

If, with my understanding of someone else, I penetrate more deeply into him, into his horizon of ownness, I shall soon run into the fact that, just as his animate bodily organism lies in my field of perception, so my animate organism lies in his field of perception and that, in general, he experiences me forthwith as an Other for him, just as I experience him as *my* Other (Husserl, Fifth Cartesian Meditation, 1960: 128–9, emphasis in original).

It follows from Husserl's statement that turn-taking can serve as evidence of an Other. Taking another into account presupposes an Other who can be taken into account.

To further illustrate turn-taking in the data presented herein would require considerable repetition. Here I simply suggest that the data provided can also be read in that way (e.g., face-to-face *interaction* with a sniper, *exchange* of gunfire, police efforts to *bait* the sniper). For those who choose to so read the data, I provide a few orienting ideas.

Sniping, at least when the target is a living being, involves turn-taking, for sniping presupposes intentionality, "shooting *at*," and a response from the one shot at. When the Other is defined as a sniper, the sniper's "turn" is especially consequential. Anyone who is in a position to see or hear a sniper, anyone whose "animate orgánism lies in his field of perception," is also in a position both to be seen and heard by the sniper *and to be shot at*. Police and civilians routinely took cover in anticipation of the sniper's turn—gunshots. Civilians and police who were wounded made the claim that they were shot *at*. Gunshots imply shooters (unless, of course, a gun goes off by accident) and being shot or shot at can serve as powerful evidence of both a sniper and of oneself as an intended target. At times police actively solicited the sniper's turn, firing at him and also yelling epithets. The sniper's availing himself of his turn would serve as evidence of his existence, although his failure to do so need not indicate nonexistence; if the existence of an Other is *assumed*, silence can be viewed as a turn.

That the second sniper not only existed but also was both aware of and acted towards those who saw or heard him[8] was described by participants and seen as consequential to them. Some "turns" were certainly attributed to Essex, but, both before and after Essex's death, other "turns" were attributed to a second sniper. Throughout the data are indications of what could count as the second sniper's "turn."

Leavings

Cultural objects "refer us to subjects" (Husserl, Fifth Cartesian Meditation, 1960: 92). After Essex's death and the identification and securing of the scene, attention turned to those cultural objects whose presence (or absence) could be taken to be signs of an Other. Elsewhere I have referred to such "leavings" as disembodied evidence.[9]

> By "disembodied" I mean to direct attention to phenomena that, at the time when they serve as evidence, are not directly attached to the bodies of individuals. By "evidence" I mean to indicate that these phenomena are used as a basis for drawing inferences about happenings in and features of the world. By the term "disembodied evidence" I wish to call attention to the processes whereby inanimate elements are "read" as evidence. "Disembodied evidence" refers to any phenomenon assigned to the physical world as it is used to make inferences about doings in and characteristics of the social world (Waksler, 1991).

A range of disembodied evidence was linked to Essex and, at least potentially, to a second sniper, serving to support the postulation of that second sniper, although in time such evidence increasingly came to be linked to Essex alone.

After Essex's death on the roof of Howard Johnson's, under his hand there was only one weapon, a .44-caliber magnum Ruger carbine, and some ammunition. "In the baggy cargo pockets of his [Essex's] fatigue pants, police said, were round cherry bombs and firecrackers, along with spare ammunition" (S-I, 1/15/73, byline John Kifner, *New York Times*). Analysis focused on the question: What is one person capable of leaving behind? Could other items, once they were deemed evidence, be linked to Essex alone or was the presence of another person, specifically another sniper, necessary to make sense of the found evidence, especially the amount? "Many of the men passing through the command post expressed amazement about the amount of ammunition the snipers possessed on the rooftop bastion" (S-I 1/8/73, byline Jack Dempsey). If there were only one sniper, that amazement would have to increase.

Particular attention focused on firearms and ammunition. Alex Vega, New Orleans Police Department's firearms identification officer,

> said there were several hundred shell cases on the roof of the building. . . . While the weapon [the Ruger carbine] is accurate at 200 to 250 yards, it is still deadly up to 1,000 yards, according to Vega. The weapon was equipped with a standard sight—no telescopic sight. . . . He said the rifle could be reloaded very quickly (S-I, 1/10/73b, byline Lanny Thomas).

Could one weapon account for all the shooting? New Orleans Police Chief Giarrusso said that

> 'spent .44 caliber magnum cartridges found on levels from which it is definitely known that a sniper fired and shell casings found on the roof area were fired by the rifle found by Essex's body. In total, a minimum of 83 .44 caliber magnum bullets were recovered, 51 of which were fired' (T-P, 2/20/73).

Ballistics evidence began to point in the direction of a single sniper. Purchase of the .44-caliber magnum was traced to Essex. "A police ballistics expert had previously linked the .44-caliber rifle found near Essex's body on Jan. 8, and registered to him, to all the shootings in both incidents [Central Lockup and Howard Johnson's]" (T-P, 2/20/73).

By 1/9/73 the link between the Central Lockup and Howard Johnson's events had been established. "Bullets from the same weapon used by the sniper in the Howard Johnson's Motor Hotel incident killed Police Cadet Alfred Harrell and wounded Patrolman Edwin S. Hosli Sr. New Year's Eve" (S-I, 1/9/73). Although the link between Essex and the gun purchase and between the gun and the spent cartridges and shell casings can be taken to be strong evidence for a single sniper, the possibility remained that among the traces of fired police weapons would be evidence indicating another sniper. It is also possible to speculate that two snipers shared the rifle, though shooting by snipers from two different places at the same time with the same weapon would undermine such a suggestion.

There were, however, reports of both the sighting and hearing of other kinds of guns (e.g., shotgun, handgun) attributed to a sniper. Robert Beamish, a hotel guest who had been shot, said that doctors "told him he had been shot in the abdomen with a 30.06-caliber rifle" (T-P, 1/10/73, byline Eric Newhouse, AP), but "Maj. Henry Morris, police chief of detectives, said yesterday the bullet that wounded Beamish was not recovered, making it impossible to prove he had been shot with a 30.06" (S-I, 1/12/73). Morris said "that there 'has been no evidence to indicate that anyone shot by a sniper at the Howard Johnson was hit by anything other than a .44-magnum slug'" (T-P, 1/12/73, byline Vincent Lee). Nonetheless,

> Suppose ballistics tests on bullets taken from other victims show they too were shot with the same weapon. Would this be strong enough evidence to conclude there was only one sniper? Would it have been possible for Essex to do all the shooting? Some people say no (S-I, 1/10/73a, byline Lanny Thomas).

Although ballistics evidence could not confirm the existence of a second sniper, neither was it adequate to rule out that possibility.[10]

Evidence for a second sniper was also sought in records of those registered in the hotel.

> There is an unconfirmed report that Essex registered at Howard Johnson's the day before the shootings started with three friends and six pieces of luggage...(ABC-TV, 1/10/73, 5:13 p.m.).

> Police said yesterday they have obtained the Howard Johnson's registry and are checking guests, raising the question whether Essex might have had someone with him who had taken a room at the hotel (S-I, 1/11/73, byline Angus Lind).

> Giarrusso would not say what evidence the police had that Essex could have been part of a plot to kill New Orleans police officers. However, he indicated that part of this evidence was the arranging of a room for Essex at the Howard Johnson Motor Lodge by someone else (S-I, 1/10/73b).

According to Maj. Henry Morris, police chief of detectives, "No suitcases, bags or cache of ammunition believed hidden by Essex were found on the roof or in the hotel" (S-I, 1/12/73a). Their presence might have supported the existence of a second sniper, but their absence left the issue open. There was no later public confirmation or refutation of Essex's either registering at the hotel or having a room taken for him by someone else, although one witness did so testify.

Once police had identified Essex, his apartment was searched. Found was a map of the city.

> Lines and circles drawn on the map included what police feel was Essex's escape route after police cadet Alfred Harrell Jr., a black, was killed New Year's Eve. . . .Central Lockup adjoins police headquarters. From that circle on the map, dashes led to the area where Patrolman Edwin Hosli was critically wounded. . . .Another circle in red was around the site of grocery store where Joseph S. Perniciaro was shot and wounded. . . .The longest line drawn on the map led from Essex's apartment to the Downtown Howard Johnson Hotel (T-P, 1/16/73).

Again the evidence did not confirm that Essex worked alone, but no evidence for the existence of another was suggested.

Looking at the shootings at Central Lockup and Howard Johnson's as elements in a single event, the number of items left behind might, or might not, be used to support the existence of a second sniper. After the shooting on 12/31/72, in the area outside the Central Lockup, police found "six spent .44 caliber magnum shell casings, one .38 caliber blue steel revolver, a four-inch barrel with the serial number filed off, five live .44 caliber magnum cartridges, a string of fire crackers and a MSA gas mask face piece and nose" (T-P, 2/20/73). In the search of warehouses across the highway from Central Lockup the police found "a brown leather bag containing two cans of lighter fluid, a 65-foot roll of bell wire and six live .44 caliber magnum cartridges" (T-P, 2/20/73) as well as "a tan long-sleeve corduroy shirt, a gas mask canister, a two-cell flashlight, a pair of cloth gloves, a leather pouch containing one box of 50 rounds of .38 caliber cartridges, a cloth sack containing 71 rounds of .38 caliber cartridges and one .44 caliber magnum cartridge" (T-P, 2/20/73). On Wednesday evening, 1/3/73, at The First New St. Mark Baptist Church, police found "a cloth sack filled with .38-caliber rounds [and] bloodstains on several doors and window sills" as well as "a note found lying near the altar" that began "'I am sorry for breaking the lock on your church door'" (Hernon, 1978/2001: 86). Two blocks from Central Lockup police also found a car registered to Essex, "a name that [at the time] was checked, cleared, and, for the time being, forgotten" (Hernon, 1978/2001: 59). On 1/10/73 police rediscovered Essex's car. In it were "about one-half ounce of marijuana," two "partially smoked marijuana cigarettes," "printed material relating to grievances against employers due to race discrimination," and "an olive-green duffel bag on which the word 'WARRIOR' was handprinted in black ink" (Hernon, 1978/2001: 259–60).

Could one person leave this number of cultural objects behind? In the absence of a second sniper, the answer would have to be yes, but when the possibility of a second sniper was still at issue, disembodied evidence provided neither support nor refutation for a second sniper. Ultimately the items left behind were inconclusive, their reading dependent on the account being offered.

Speculation and Conspiracy Theories

During the event, in the face of incomplete, ambiguous, and conflicting information, both the police and the public sought understanding. Into the gap came "improvised news" (Shibutani, 1966), speculation about how the event was unfolding and why. Some of that speculation was based on the *assumption* of the existence of more than one sniper.

A veteran police officer said, "you'll find they were all ex-combat servicemen" (S-I 1/8/73, byline Jack Dempsey). Describing the assault on the roof bunker, Reporter Bill Crider refers to "the strange *suicide squad of snipers*— who seemed to come from nowhere with no known motive" (S-I, 1/8/73, byline Bill Crider, AP, emphasis added). Once they were described as a "suicide squad of snipers," evasive tactics could be attributed to them to account even for the *absence* of sightings. Crider quotes one of the helicopter gunners, "'I just don't see how they can survive those ricochets'" but, Crider continues, "They did it, it developed, by ducking part-way down the stairs when the chopper loomed out of the mist..." (S-I, 1/8/73, byline Bill Crider, AP). Thus Crider describes not being able to see the snipers as *confirmation* of not only their expertise but of their very presence.

An unsubstantiated television report speculated about the snipers' plan, saying, "the two alleged accomplices were to set fires throughout the hotel and then escape as guests fled. Essex's job was to stay behind and carry out the sniping attack alone, the report added, dying if necessary" (T-P, 1/16/73). Another newspaper report offers an account of events after Essex's death:

> After a night of intermittent gunfire, the remaining two snipers apparently separated, taking up positions at either end of the hotel rooftop. One appeared to have been forced down a stairwell onto a ledge above the 18th floor but they still had enough firepower to wound three policemen aboard a helicopter as it made an early-morning pass over the rooftop (S-I, 1/8/73a).

The wounding of three policemen after Essex's death strongly supported speculation about the existence of at least one other sniper.

Resources available to the snipers were also postulated. "If the sniper or snipers had a radio, it would have been easy to monitor the police radio band. In some instances, they could have learned a lot about police plans by monitoring the commercial radio and television stations" (S-I, 1/12/73, byline Allan Katz).

Conspiracy theories were put forth. Sniping, killing police, and killing whites were taken to be the kinds of things that a militant black conspiracy might do. Such theories were substantiated in part by recent local events.

> New Orleans police already had endured two stand-offs with members of he Black Panther Party in the Desire public housing complex. And other left-wing groups were still around from the heyday of radical protests in the 1960s, including many committed to violence as an avenue to social change (T-P, 1/7/98, byline Dennis Persica).

> A week before. . .New Orleans police received word to be on the lookout for four men wanted in connection with the shooting of six Detroit policemen last month. . . .There is no evidence of a connection. . . (S-I, 1/8/73b).

In the early phases of the event, "Police Supt. Clarence Giarrusso attributes the attacks to a 'well planned' assassination and points to 'overtones of a militant group'" (S-I, 1/8/73, byline Ray Lincoln).

Conspiracy theories both supported the idea of more than one sniper and allowed for the linking of previous and ongoing events. A timeline offered by reporter Ray Lincoln on 1/8/73 included as potentially related to the event at the Howard Johnson's Motel a series of fatal fires in New Orleans in the previous year and a half, including the Rault Center fire on 11/29/72. However, "Fire chief Louis San Salvador said the recent outbreak of fires here are the result of arson, but he sees no connection among the blazes" (S-I, 1/9/73d).

A range of public officials offered conspiracy theories that went beyond the local to the national. State Atty. General William J. Guste was quoted as saying, "I am now convinced that there is an underground national suicidal group bent on creating terror in America" (S-I, 1/9/73, byline Ray Lincoln). Sen. James O. Eastland, D–Miss., said the incident was "ample evidence that a nationwide conspiracy exists to kill policemen" (S-I, 1/9/73e). Dr. Guy Gibson, director of the local branch of the NAACP,

> attributed the incident to 'some determined radicals, maybe motivated—not only motivated, but planned and executed—by some national group. It may have involved some local citizens, but only a very minute number,' he said (S-I, 1/10/73, byline Patsy Sims).

Identification of a national conspiracy would have practical consequences: it could, for example, be used to bring in federal resources. Irvin Magri, head of the Patrolman's Association of New Orleans, said, "the attack on New Orleans policemen no longer is a local problem, but is part of a national conspiracy that requires federal help" (S-I, 1/12/73b) and "Atty. Gen. William Guste has renewed his appeal to the federal government to investigate the Jan. 7 sniper attack at the downtown Howard Johnson's Motor Lodge to determine whether a national conspiracy was involved" (S-I, 1/22/73).

As the event was drawing to a close, Police Chief Giarrusso said, "'No evidence has been produced to link Essex. . .with any militant or insurrective organizations'" (S-I, 1/10/73a, byline Lanny Thomas). A later status report by the New Orleans Police Department states, "'There is no substantial evidence that Essex's acts were a part of [or] extension of revolutionary programs'" (S-I, 2/20/73, byline Allan Katz). Evidence gathered later failed to support any of the conspiracy theories, despite the certainty and conviction with which they were initially offered.

In the search for an explanation of the events at the time they were unfolding, however, conspiracy theories and general speculation provided ways to deal with the events as a meaningful whole. And conspiracy theories added weight to the existence of at least a second sniper. Governor Edwin Edwards, offering alternative possibilities, was quoted as saying it had to be either "a conspiracy or the product of a diseased and criminal mind" (S-I, 1/9/73, byline Ray Lincoln). In the midst of the event, the actions of a conspiracy might offer more guidelines for response than would "a diseased and criminal mind."

WHAT ONE PERSON IS CAPABLE OF DOING: THE "ESCAPE" OF THE SECOND SNIPER

On the Monday afternoon after Essex's death, police carried out an assault on the rooftop bunker, "thought to be the last possible hiding place" for a second sniper (CBS-TV, 1/8/73, 5:30 p.m.). The event was carried live on television, suggesting the general expectation that a second sniper would be discovered. When he was not, there was surprise and confusion.

Attention then turned to the heating and cooling system, deemed once again the last possible hiding place. "The hotel architect told reporters. . .'If they get into the heating and air-conditioning ducts, they can get anywhere in the building'" (S-I, 1/10/73b). "The [air conditioning] vents are rather small but then the second sniper could have been rather small too" (NBC-TV, 1/9/73, 5:31 p.m.). Police Superintendent Giarrusso said, "He [a second sniper] believed to be hiding in one of the hotel's air conditioning ducts could be out of the building or could still be hiding in it" (T-P, 1/9/73, byline J.E. Bourgoyne). "Eventually they [police] would search the air-conditioning ducts and machinery and nooks and crannies along the roof and tear out the false ceilings in the hotel bathrooms. They found no one" (S-I, 1/15/73, byline John Kifner, *New York Times*). In the words of a TV reporter, "The danger of a second sniper has vanished. For that matter, the second sniper himself has vanished. . ." (NBC-TV, 1/9/73, 5:31 p.m.). What could be concluded from the continuing absence of a second sniper? Either the second sniper had escaped or there had never been more than one sniper.

At this point the existence of an Other turns from physical evidence—sightings, hearings, leavings—to logic: *How* could a second sniper escape? At first it was claimed that escape was impossible.

> David Huber, a police sharpshooter who spent Monday night and all day yesterday on the chilly rooftop[11], was convinced there was only one sniper and that nobody escaped. . . .'There's no way he (a second sniper) could have gotten off the roof. All three exits were blocked and the 18th floor was completely sealed off' (S-I, 1/9/73, byline Angus Lind).

> Giarrusso. . .said policemen have insisted to him that they had the roof 'adequately sealed off' and that there was no way for a sniper to

escape. All exists were covered, he said (S-I, 1/10/73a, byline Lanny Thomas).

Nonetheless, the possibility of escape was entertained.

> [I]n reading the building plans, the police did not notice a stairway that leads from the maid's storage room next to the elevators on the 18th floor up to the inside of the rooftop mechanical building. Apparently they did not learn of this until early Monday, when told of it by an engineer (S-I, 1/15/73, byline John Kifner, *New York Times*).

> [Giarrusso] acknowledged the possibility, heretofore denied, that a second sniper slipped out of the heavily guarded hotel. The superintendent said there was a 'space of time' before the police could get a copy of the building's plans and found out there was a way to get from the motor lodge to a nearby building. Under more questioning, Giarrusso identified the 'unobvious exit' as the elevator shaft. Newsmen inside the hotel said police didn't begin guarding the bottom of the elevator shaft until after sunrise Monday (S-I, 1/10/73b).

The elevators stopped working some time before 11:00 a.m. on Sunday, when the fires in the hotel began. For a half hour or more Police Officers Michael Burl and Robert Childress were trapped in an elevator at the 18th floor. In order to escape the heavy smoke, they opened the trap door at the top of the elevator and slid down the cable eighteen floors. Thereafter, guarding the elevator shaft might have seemed of lower priority than guarding the stairwells, though, given the police officers' actions, a sniper could conceivably have followed their route.

Later interviews with police witnesses suggested that, although officers were assigned to guard the stairwells, there were gaps in the coverage. On the morning of 1/8, for example, "it was noted that some of the floors were not guarded as they were the previous day, and Lt. O'Donnell then assigned officers to these areas" (Det. Robert Pointevent, PR: 542).

Even were a route out of the hotel available, there were clear risks to using it. On 1/15/73, a week after the event, a reporter asked, "Was there more than one sniper? If so, how was an escape made past a swarm of 600 heavily armed policemen in and around the hotel?" (S-I, 1/15/73, byline John Kifner, *New York Times*). One possible answer: "Some individuals have speculated that if there were indeed two or more snipers, they might have changed into police uniforms and walked past the officers" (S-I, 1/10/73a, byline Lanny Thomas). "Asked at his joint news conference with Mayor Moon Landrieu how a second sniper could have gotten away, Giarrusso said: 'There's a gamut of possibilities, ranging from police negligence to a superbrain sniper" (S-I, 1/9/73b).

The continued failure to find an embodied Other, i.e., a second sniper, or reliable sightings of an *escaping* sniper, as well as the difficulty (albeit not impossibility) of escape, led increasingly to the conclusion that there had been no

Other, and thus no Other to have escaped. If, however, there had only been one sniper, what was to be done with all the evidence of that second sniper? I address that topic in the next chapter. First, however, I turn to a brief consideration of ambiguous evidence assessed in terms of "common sense."

A NOTE ON AMBIGUITY: EITHER/OR EXPLANATIONS

Throughout the accounts of the event, intriguing dichotomous explanations are offered that indicate attempts to reconcile evidence and common sense. Some explanations are of the form: A is obviously true, B is obviously false (or at least unlikely). Police Superintendent Giarrusso said, "I've got to assume that the policemen did see something. I can't believe that all the policemen who formed the defense perimeter were hallucinating" (T-P, 1/10/73, byline Emile LaFourcade). Assessing probabilities Giarrusso said,

> I've got to assume that police saw something. . . .After the death of the man, the plane was fired upon. One would have to assume that the police hit the plane. This is possible but, in my opinion, highly improbable (ABC-TV, 19/73, 5:12 p.m.).

Giarrusso said that "after Essex was shot, several policemen saw another person on the roof and 'there were very, very many shots taken at this person while this person *or this ghost* allegedly moved" (T-P, 1/10/73, byline Emile LaFourcade, emphasis added).

Yet other explanations juxtaposed equally unlikely options.

> Only the body of the sniper killed last night by police gunfire was found on the roof. Either the other sniper or snipers escaped, or there was only one gunman in the first place. The latter appeared impossible, since police have taken return fire several times since the first gunman was slain. Three policemen were injured by gunfire this morning. Escape also seemed unlikely, since police have had the 18th floor secured and guarded since early today (S-I, 1/8/73a).

> If there was nothing to be found here [in the air conditioning system] or anywhere in the building, it meant that a sniper had escaped through a motel filled with police or that there'd never been more than one sniper and the sniper fire after his death was imagined by officers, one conclusion as incredible as another (CBS-TV, 1/8/73, 5:30 p.m.).

> It seems to be very difficult to accept the idea that just one man could have set these fires, caused such a panic, and stood off the entire police department of the city of New Orleans but it seems equally hard to accept the idea that that same man [sic] could get out of the building when it was occupied by hundreds of policemen (NBC-TV, 1/9/73, 5:31 p.m.).

When the only available explanations are rejected, where is explanation to be sought? Deliberations continued.

> He [Giarrusso] said that after several skull sessions with his officers and giving the matter some deep thought over Monday night, 'I have found several indications leading to there being a second person on the roof, but I have also come up with several things to indicate that Essex had no help' (T-P, 1/10/73, byline Emile LaFourcade).

Either/or explanations, especially when they juxtapose equally unlikely possibilities, serve to set the problem in stark relief. Resolution awaited the reassessment of available evidence and the gathering of new evidence in order to choose among alternatives or to identify other possibilities.

LEGITIMATING EVIDENCE

At the time of the event and afterwards, evidence was assessed and legitimated not only in terms of its content but also in relation to *who* offered it. That offered by police seemed to have de facto legitimation simply because it was presented by police–although later it too was subject to question. Initially,

> Giarrusso said he has no reason to doubt policemen who said they saw someone 'moving' on the building and the other officers near the roof who said they heard 'talking and shouting' (S-I, 1/10/73a, byline Lanny Thomas).

In time he did have such reason, leaving him with the dilemma of how to discount "reliable police reports" without compromising either those who made them or the legitimacy of police procedures in general. Giarrusso stated, "Police have given conflicting statements as to what they saw and heard" (S-I, 1/10/73a, byline Lanny Thomas). Inevitably some reports would be deemed true, others false. Those whose evidence was discounted had their sense experiences and their common-sense reasoning denigrated.

Some civilians who offered evidence presented it with accompanying legitimation. Hotel guest Beamish and reporter McMillan offered credentials for the validity of their evidence. The former cited the length of his observations: He "stared at his assailant until he was shot, then watched him intermittently from a distance for more than three hours" (T-P, 1/10/73, byline Eric Newhouse, AP). McMillan offered confirmation of his experiences by citing others who were with him. For reporter Manguno, the confirmation of what he heard and saw by others present, and policemen at that, served as substantiation of his claims. (See above, pp. 26–27, for McMillan and Manguno's statements.)

At the time of the event reporters described informants in ways that seemed to offer support for the legitimacy of their claims: "a prominent New Orleans businessman," "a police officer," "sheriff's deputy," "police chaplain," etc. One piece of evidence that placed Essex elsewhere than at the hotel at the beginning of the event was simply described (and perhaps delegitimized) as offered by

"Edwin L. Wilson, 76" (the only time I noted an age and no other identifying information given for a witness; for his statement, see p. 17).

Those who had face-to-face interactions with a sniper (hotel employees and guests) might be thought to offer especially legitimate evidence, but in time their claims came in for reassessment. Those who identified photos of Essex were deemed reliable, but those who could not identify a photo of Essex or identified a photo of someone else compromised the claim that there had been but one sniper—unless their claims could somehow be discounted.

Given the absence of incontrovertible evidence that there was a second sniper–e.g., a physical body either dead or alive–the existence of that Other remained inferential, neither confirmed nor refuted. In the aftermath, efforts were directed to gathering further information to be used in supplementing evidence available at the time of the event and reassessing its legitimacy. As the postulation of a second sniper lost credence, emphasis turned to attributing more and more evidence to Essex. For evidence that could not be so linked, alternative explanations were sought that did not postulate a second sniper.

NOTES

1. "Ordinary" or "normal" is obviously a social construction. Such construction is exemplified in data I collected on deviance in a kindergarten classroom (Waksler, 1987). Certain of children's actions were met with the teacher's comment, "People don't do that." Thus children were being instructed in what "people do." The actions that brought this response indicate the teacher's power (and perhaps idiosyncrasies) in defining "normality." Such sanctionable actions by children included pouting, rolling on the floor, ripping a book, and dancing when the music was over. Those who witnessed or reported on the New Orleans sniper(s) came to the event with ideas of what an ordinary person could and could not do.

2. I found no further reference to this report or any evidence that it was taken seriously.

3. See Chapter 4, especially the section entitled "Others are Seeable: Retrospective Sightings" and the Appendix for varying descriptions of the sniper(s).

4. Beamish, however, was under the impression that Essex was 5'4", which may have influenced his identification. He did not, however, identify a photo of Essex and said that the rifle carried by the sniper who shot him was not a .44 magnum Ruger carbine rifle. (For further details, see Appendix.)

5. It is not always clear whether "balcony" refers to the 17th floor balcony or the 8th floor patio.

6. No interviews with reporters were included in the Police Report and it is not clear whether or not the police interviewed any reporters.

7. In newspaper accounts and the Police Report, "negro" is used most frequently, followed by "colored" and, rarely, "black." (In 1973 New Orleans, "African-American" may not have been widely used.) I have used "black" to remain somewhat within this terminological framework.

8. I refer to the second sniper as "him" since, with a few problematic exceptions, witnesses' descriptions of a purported second sniper were of a male.

9. What I have termed "disembodied evidence" is a concept that draws on Goffman's concepts of "embodied information" and "disembodied messages." Goffman states,

> The information that an individual provides, whether he sends it or exudes it, may be *embodied* or *disembodied*. . . .Disembodied messages, such as the ones we receive from letters and mailed gifts, or the ones hunters receive from the spoor of a now distant animal, require that the organism do something that traps and holds information long after the organism has stopped informing. This study will be concerned only with embodied information (1963: 14, emphasis in original).

Goffman did not concern himself with disembodied evidence; I have done so in an unpublished paper entitled "Disembodied Evidence: The Social Significance of Inanimate Phenomena" (1991). My ideas about disembodied evidence have guided my claims in this section.

10. According to the Police Report, five bullets removed from victims could be linked to Essex's rifle; no ballistics information is provided from other victims.

11. The building is not specified. Police had taken positions on the roofs of a number of nearby buildings.

CHAPTER 4.
THE AFTERMATH:
UNCONSTITUTING THE OTHER

After a final room-by-room search of Howard Johnson's, the quest for definitive evidence of the existence or nonexistence of a second sniper turned to a review of radio tapes and to interviews with police, firefighters, hotel employees, hotel guests, and others. For some time the postulation of a second sniper remained viable.

> A reconstruction of the shootout and the events leading up to it—based on interviews with the police, witnesses and other informed sources—indicates the following: There were probably at least two additional persons—a black man and a black woman—involved in the shootout. . . .There are strong indications the Howard Johnson's shootings were planned in advance, with ammunition having been taken previously into the hotel. The snipers may have rented a room over the weekend (S-I, 1/15/73, byline John Kifner, *New York Times*).

By January 25, however, the idea that there was a second sniper was losing credence. Work began to transmute the second sniper into what Husserl (see below) terms a "pseudo-organism."

The assumption that there was more than one sniper, plausible as it was at first, as well as useful in terms of public safety, came to be seen as both troublesome and increasingly implausible. Given that neither the second sniper nor unambiguous evidence of that sniper could be found, what was to be done with what previously counted as evidence for his existence? Work proceeded to "lose" the second sniper. The "losing," however, was carried out in such a way that the reasonableness of the initial postulation was to some extent preserved, for the alternative was to fault a number of others who, apparently in good faith, offered and acted on contradictory evidence.

Husserl writes,

> Regarding experiences of someone else, it is clear that its fulfillingly verifying continuation can ensue *only by means of new appresentations that proceed in a synthetically harmonious fashion*, and only by virtue of the manner in which *these appresentations owe their existence-value to their motivational connexion with the* changing *presentations proper, within my ownness*, that continually appertain to them. . . .The experienced animate organism of another continues to prove itself as actually an animate organism, solely in its changing but incessantly *harmonious 'behavior'*. . . .The organism becomes experienced as a pseudo-organism, precisely if there is something discordant about its behavior (Fifth Cartesian Meditation, 1960: 114, emphasis in original).

The search for a second sniper through "new appresentations that proceed in a synthetically harmonious fashion" met with many obstacles. Particularly "discordant about its [his] behavior" were his unexplained disappearance and the absence of *incontrovertible* evidence of his very existence. Investigation then turned to reconstituting Mark Essex as the *only* sniper. The process entailed in part the reassigning to Essex of elements that were initially attributed to a second sniper.

REWORKING THE EVIDENCE

If there had been no second sniper, how could the evidence for that second sniper be reinterpreted or discounted? With the continued absence of an Other (a second sniper), attention turned to an explanation that would satisfactorily account for there never having been more than one sniper, Essex.

> Is there any entity in itself so indubitably certain to me through immediate experience that I could, in accord with this experience, with descriptive concepts which immediately fit this experience or the content of this experience, express immediate truths in themselves? But what about any and every experience of what is in the world, experience of what I am immediately certain of as existing spatiotemporally? It is certain; but this certainty can modalize itself, it can become doubtful, it can dissolve in the course of experience into illusion; no immediate experiential assertion gives me an entity as what it is in itself but only something meant with certainty that must verify itself in the course of my experiencing life. But the verification which lies merely in the harmonious character of actual experience does not prevent the possibility of illusion (Husserl, n.d.: 335).

> Thus, in the case of evidence of immanent data, I can return to them in a series of intuitive recollections that has the open endlessness which the 'I can always do so again' (as a horizon of potentiality) creates. Without such 'possibilities' there would be for us no *fixed and abiding* being, no real and no ideal world. Both of these exist for us thanks to evidence or the presumption of being able to make evi-

dent and to repeat acquired evidence (Husserl, Third Cartesian Meditation, 1960: 60).

The repetition of "acquired evidence" of a second sniper, however, proved problematic. Previous evidence came in for reinterpretation, guided by new information. "I can always do so again" was replaced with "I can now do so differently." Attention returned to the evidence used to constitute a second sniper. Efforts were directed to explaining *away* the evidence for the second sniper by discounting or refuting that evidence or providing alternative explanations that did not involve a second sniper. New evidence was gathered and previous evidence reinterpreted and redistributed, some to Essex, some to faulty reasoning, some to the general confusion. The process began haltingly shortly after the event; by the time of the August 31 New Orleans Police Department Report, the process was largely complete and there was general agreement that there had only been one sniper. Nonetheless, some doubts remained, some questions unanswered.

The search for confirmation of a second sniper had been repeatedly unsuccessful. Once Essex was identified, one place where evidence for a second sniper was sought was in Essex's biography. "The investigation, at this point, seems to be concerned with what motivated Essex. Was he part of a suicide pact with a mission, or was he just a loner bent on killing policemen and firemen?" (S-I, 1/10/73a, byline Lanny Thomas). "[F]acts about the dead sniper's past may shed some light on how many gunmen were involved" (S-I, 1/10/73a, byline Lanny Thomas).

A friend of Essex's was reported as saying that Essex was not a member of any militant organization (CBS-TV, 1/10/73, 5:48 p.m.), suggesting that he could have acted alone. A search of Essex's apartment, however, disclosed walls covered with what could be described as "militant slogans."

> The words 'hate' and 'kill' were splashed everywhere, seemingly at random. Next to the word 'Africa' was scrawled, 'Hate white people—beast of the earth.' Inside the giant C of 'AFRICA' Essex had carefully penciled in, 'The quest for freedom is death—then by death I shall escape to freedom.' Near the ceiling was spelled out, 'The third World—Kill Pig Nixon and all his running dogs.' No inch of wall space was spared; lifting their heads, detectives saw in bold red letters, 'Only a pig would read shit on the ceiling' (Hernon, 1978/2001: 262).

Nonetheless, "It's not certain, of course, that Essex himself did all this [writing on walls] but it was done since he rented the apartment" (CBS-TV, 1/12/73, 5:36 p.m.).

> Throughout this entire investigation into the background of Mark Essex, no firm, physical evidence was found which would link him to any of the known subversive or militant groups, although his possible

involvement with several such groups was hinted by more than one source interviewed (PR: 241).

The absence of any direct links to militant groups supported the idea that Essex acted alone and, further, provided no leads for seeking a second sniper.

Evidence pointing to Essex alone continued to amass. A significant piece of new information emerged:

> On or about January 3, 1973, an envelope addressed to WWL-TV was received by that station. . . .It was finally opened [on January 6 or 7]. . .and delivered to the Intelligence Division of the New Orleans Police Department. . .on January 12. . . .[T]he postmark on the envelope is January 2. . . .Handwriting experts assigned to the Crime Lab have established that the handwriting on this letter is of the same authorship as other samples of handwriting bearing the signature of Mark J. Essex (PR: 288–9).

The letter read:

> Africa greets you. . . .on Dec 31 1972 appt [sic] 11 the Downtown New Orleans Police Dept will be attack. . .Reason — many. . . .But the death of two innocent [sic] brothers will be avenged. And many others. . .P.S. tell Pig Gurrusso [sic] the felony action squad [aint] shit. . . MATA (PR: 288).[1]

Even in light of the new evidence being amassed, Giarrusso continued to maintain that "it has not been definitely determined if Essex did or did not have one or more accomplices or co-conspirators in the criminal acts committed on those two dates" (T-P, 2/20/73). The continued failure to find such associates, however, while strengthening the possibility of their being a single sniper, merely weakened rather than refuted the possibility of a second sniper.

As new evidence continued to undermine the idea of a second sniper, at least by failing to support it, earlier evidence, gathered when the existence of a second sniper was *assumed* and supporting that assumption, was reassessed. How could evidence be reassigned to unconstitute the Other? The very features that were used to constitute the second sniper came to be used to unconstitute that sniper. The features held; their empirical referents changed.

NOPD REPORT[2]

The August 31, 1973 New Orleans Police Department "Report Relating to the Homicide Investigation Conducted into the Criminal Activities of Mark J. Essex, Jr., Age 23, Formerly Residing 2619-1/2 Dryades Street" describes the NOPD investigation which "began on Sunday, December 31, 1972[3] and was actively pursued into the early part of August, 1973" (1). (All references in the remainder of this chapter are to this Report unless otherwise noted). The 889-page Report describes "a careful examination of each crime scene and the subsequent location and identification of physical evidence, which prove beyond any doubt that Mark Essex was the perpetrator of the several crimes described throughout this report" (3).

The Report makes clear the enormity of the task facing the police, both at the time of the event and in its aftermath, and the many resources that they brought to bear as they sought to make sense of the event as a whole. That some matters remain unexplained is not a criticism of the Report or the police; rather it is an inevitable result of the extreme complexity of the event and the limits of the police mandate. In what follows I am not engaging in police work but in phenomenological analysis. For the police, unconstituting the second sniper was taken to follow from the context within which they were working and the evidence available to them. My quite different goal is to understand *how* unconstituting was accomplished. That process, as well as lingering traces of a second sniper, are phenomenologically interesting without necessarily being relevant to or critical of the work of the police.

The Report itself creates a strong framework for the conclusion that there was only one sniper. The very title of the report presupposes that Essex was the only sniper. The Introduction ends with the statement: "Mark Essex acted alone in carrying out his mission of terror, destruction, and death" (5). In telling the story with Essex as the only sniper, the Report itself makes an important contribution to unconstituting the second sniper. Contradictory evidence is presented in ways that allow the story of a single sniper to hold. As the story unfolds, linking abundant evidence to Essex, the space that might be occupied by a second sniper contracts significantly. Nonetheless, that space, constricted as it is, does remain.

Early in the Report mention is made of "sniper(s)," but soon the story becomes a story of Essex. The Time Sequence Outline says of the January 1 break-in at the church, "*Mark Essex* forcibly entered the church and hid there" (28, emphasis added). The Narrative states of the period after the shooting at Central Lockup (12/31 to 1/1), "From all indications, it would appear that *Essex* fled from the rear window of the warehouse, alongside the railroad tracks, across Earhart Boulevard on South Lopez Street, where he found refuge inside the First New St. Mark Baptist Church, at least until the evening of 1/1 when Reverend Williams returned to the church and surprised him" (64, emphasis added). It is noteworthy here that Reverend Williams says in his interview that he could not positively identify a photo of Essex.

When the Time Sequence Outline and Narrative turn specifically to the events at Howard Johnson's, references throughout are to the activities of Essex, a single sniper, acting alone. For example, "Mark Essex abandoned the stolen vehicle on the 4th level of the parking garage. . ." (73); and "Upon seeing that police officers were guarding the car [that Essex was said to have stolen and that was in the 4th floor parking garage] he fired once through the glass window in the stairwell door at them" (115).

Claims of sightings of Essex, rather than of an unidentified sniper, are made even when witnesses do not identify Essex from photos. Thus, the Narrative states that hotel guest Wallace Johnson "saw Mark Essex carrying a rifle come out a room on the 11th floor to his left" (87) although Johnson "described Essex as a negro male, attired in a leather jacket, but was unable to give any further description" (88). Johnson thus claims that he saw a person but does not claim that he saw *Essex*. Similarly,

> Mrs. Calloway saw Mark Essex, carrying a rifle, walk onto the balcony near the room that was burning. Mrs. Calloway was unable to identify photographs of Mark Essex because she could only see his upper torso and the rifle that he was carrying (89).

> [Police] Sgt. Glen Keller related that he was on the roof of the Demontluzin Building and saw Mark Essex at the Gravier-Loyola corner of the Howard Johnson's patio area, armed with a rifle. Sgt. Keller could not see him well enough to determine if he was actually the sniper, or if he was a police officer in plainclothes (108).

In an interview in which his description of the sniper varies widely from descriptions of Essex (i.e., as a 5'10" white man in tight-fitting light blue clothing), Sgt. George Delpidio, Jr. nonetheless says, "I heard a shot from the area where I had last seen Essex. . . ." (381).[4] The Report even cites as observers of Essex those who deny that he was the person they saw. Thus, the Report states that Carrie Mae Clemmons, a hotel maid, "observed Mark Essex walking through the Gravier Street stairwell doorway" (85) even though "She was subsequently shown photographs of Mark Essex, but stated that he was not the subject she had seen on the 11th floor" (85).

The Time Sequence Outline and Narrative sections of the Report reframe and expand the event in time and space, linking the occurrences at Howard Johnson's to the events that began at Central Lockup on 12/31/72. Ballistics evidence served not only to connect the shooting at Central Lockup with that at Howard Johnson's–the same rifle was used at both locations–but also to provide beginning and end points to the event that could then be filled in with other evidence. Thus the event comes to be taken as beginning[5] with the sniping at Central Lockup on 12/31/72 at 10:52 p.m. (during which one police cadet was killed and a police officer wounded) and to include a break-in at the Oliver Van Horn Company; shooting at the Burkart Manufacturing Company on South Gayoso Street (at which one police officer was killed); two break-ins at The First New St. Mark Baptist Church, the first on 1/1 (first sighting of a person, "a young negro male") and the second on 1/3; a sighting on 1/2 and later shooting (not fatal) on 1/7 of the proprietor at Joe's Grocery; and ending on 1/7 at approximately 8:50 p.m. with Essex's death. The active search for a second sniper inside Howard Johnson's continued until the evening of Monday, 1/8 and interviews continued until early February, but the Report retrospectively ends the event with the death of Essex.

Thus a path in space and time was created for Essex to have followed, a process facilitated by the finding in Essex's apartment after his death of an Esso street map of New Orleans "on which Police headquarters and the downtown Howard Johnson's were circled in black. The fastest route from Essex's apartment to the hotel was overlined" (Hernon, 1978/2001: 261). As more and more evidence came to be linked to Essex, traces of a second sniper were significantly reduced. Were the existence of a second sniper to have been confirmed, some of this evidence might have been attributed to him, but the conclusion that Essex acted alone made such attribution unnecessary.

The Report acknowledges that, after Essex's death, police remained on the scene and the search for a second sniper in the hotel continued at least until the evening of Monday, 1/8. The description of this work, however, begins the process of unconstituting the second sniper by offering alternative explanations (it was "later learned" and "in later interviews").

> Because of variations in the description of the sniper during the day [Sunday], it was believed that there was more than one sniper on the premises at this time, therefore, police officers maintained their positions after Essex was fatally shot. Additionally, police officers from different vantage points reported that they could see someone moving about the area of the motel roof. Other police officers in the stairwells reported hearing voices on the roof of the motel (*later learned to be police officers on adjoining buildings*) (40, emphasis added).
>
> From approximately 8:50 PM until about 3:50 AM on January 8, 1973, several police units in the area reported seeing something that looked like a second sniper on the roof of the motel. *In later interviews* with police officers, F.B.I. agents, civilians, and the helicopter crew, it was determined that the only sniper on the roof during the entire incident was the dead sniper, Mark Essex (125).

The Report, begun with some tentativeness, early in the telling moves to a story of Essex as the only sniper. This move involves inferences drawn directly from old and new evidence (sightings, leavings, physical evidence) and the reworking of contradictory evidence. It also, and inevitably, entails new speculation to fill in the gaps. Thus the unconstituting of the second sniper begins.

WHAT ONE PERSON IS CAPABLE OF DOING: MARK ESSEX (THE "FIRST" SNIPER)

The assumption that one person could not have done what was done came in for reassessment. If all the sights, sounds, and leavings could be attributed to Essex, the space formerly inhabited by a second sniper could be eliminated, or at least significantly reduced—for that everything *could* be attributed to Essex did not prove that it had to be so attributed.

On 2/15 the police conducted two trial runs to "duplicate Essex's actions as he proceeded through the hotel and simulated the setting of fires, conversations with maids, struggle with guests, and firing the rifle" (243). Newspaper reports at the time were somewhat tentative:

> By putting the [police radio] tapes together, police now allow that just one man could have set the fires and taken shots at them by himself. Police still agree, however, that it is not inconceivable that Essex was not alone (T-P, 1/25/73).

By contrast, the Report presents the matter more definitively:

> By using the transcribed tapes of the entire radio communications and the written and verbal statement of the participants, the investigating officers were able to recreate the events of the day. After doing this, it was then necessary to prove that it was possible for Essex alone to have done what was done; this was proven by the time trial runs. . . (248).

If Essex *could* have done it all, the single-sniper theory was supported. There were, however, those who continued to reject the possibility that one person could done everything. By 2/10/73 the State Fire Marshal Raymond B. Oliver was still unconvinced.

> [He] said it was impossible for one man to have set fires on six different floors during the Jan. 7 sniping incident. . . .'T]hose fires had to be set by two or more people'. . . .'I'm telling you that you couldn't go on the eighth floor, 11th, 12th, 15th, 17th and 18th floors and set fires, and be shooting and sniping out the window at the same time' (S-I, 2/10/73).

Nonetheless, evidence increasingly was taken to support the idea of a single sniper.

One issue that came in for reworking was Essex's skill, or lack thereof. Although there was little evidence that Essex was particularly skilled—a friend of Essex's was reported as saying that Essex had no gun training (CBS-TV, 1/10/73, 5:48 p.m.)—the Report states:

> The scope of Essex's activities lends substantial credence to speculation that he was trained to accomplish what he did, trained so well, in fact, that he was able to elude pursuing police officers for over ten hours, prior to being killed. . . .While the investigation into Essex's background failed to develop the source and scope of any such training, there is some evidence to indicate that he did undergo a period of training shortly after his release from the Navy, at least there is a period of time during this period that his activities are not readily accounted for (241).

Identification of the source of such training might support this claim, but the evidence here rests on no more than "a period of time. . .that his [Essex's] activities are not readily accounted for."

Were Essex indeed skilled, the confusion during the event could at least in part be attributed to Essex:

> There can be no doubt that Essex was well trained, both in firearms and in urban guerilla tactics; his "hit and run" and "confuse the enemy" tactics are well defined in manuals and other literature printed by known subversive groups (241).

Some arguments, however, could be made that Essex was not particularly skilled, e.g., his use of pistol ammunition in his rifle.

> In a later examination of the weapon [found by Essex's body], a spent casing was found in the breech, which was a result of shooting handgun ammunition in the rifle instead of regular rifle ammunition. Firearms experts advised that this type of ammunition tends to jam in semi-automatic rifles (167).

The quantity and variety of items found and linked to Essex (see below, "Leavings") could suggest either that he was well prepared (because of what he had) or that he was very disorganized (because of what he left behind before he reached Howard Johnson's). Evidence for Essex's skill thus remains, in the absence of direct evidence, speculative at best. Nonetheless, the evidence can be read as indicating that one person *could* have done what was done.

REWORKING SIGNS OF AN OTHER

> [T]he world is our common world, necessarily having ontic validity; yet in particular matters I can enter into contradiction with others, into doubt and negation of being, similarly to the way I do this with myself. . . .[Corrected] experience—either as communal experience and reciprocal correction or as one's own personal experience and self correction—*does not change the relativity of the experience*; even as communal experience it is relative, and thus all descriptive assertions are necessarily relative, and all conceivable inferences, deductive or inductive, are relative (Husserl, n.d.: 336, emphasis added).[6]

The Report "enter[s] into contradiction with others, into doubt and negation of being" of the second sniper. The Report can be viewed as a "correction" of experience, though, as Husserl indicates, "all descriptive assertions" and "all conceivable inferences. . .are relative." Certainly some of those whose evidence was contradicted were not persuaded. Nonetheless, reworked evidence served, at least conditionally, as a basis for unconstituting the second sniper.

In unconstituting the second sniper, sights, sounds, and leavings were redistributed—some attributed to Essex, some withdrawn from him, some reassigned to police. Evidence of turn-taking was reassessed. New speculation replaced old.

The process was not unproblematic, but the *assumption* that Essex was the only sniper facilitated the reading of evidence to document that assumption.

Others are Seeable: Sightings at Howard Johnson's

Of particular importance in considering sightings is that, until Essex's death and identification, no one *saw* Essex; they saw a person who was only later determined by police–though not by all witnesses–to have been Essex. Once Essex was identified and no other sniper was discovered, police attributed all sightings in the hotel to Essex (or to police or civilians "mistakenly" identified as a sniper). Although all sightings of *Essex* were therefore retrospective, I have reserved the term "retrospective sightings" (in the next section) to call particular attention to those occurring prior to Essex's arrival at Howard Johnson's and made under quite different circumstances.

Sightings[7] of a sniper or snipers were provided by witnesses with differing vantage points. Hotel employees and guests inside the hotel described face-to-face contact with a person taken to be a sniper, some actually speaking with that person. Sightings by police were made from outside the hotel and from some distance away, e.g., from the ground or from adjacent buildings that offered vantage points of Howard Johnson's from the 8th floor to the roof. Many police reported never seeing a sniper at all.

Witnesses' claims about whom and what they saw came in for assessment and reformulation. Those whose evidence was discounted may, however, have remained unpersuaded by the new evidence.

> [T]he fact, 'I am', prescribes *whether* other monads are others for me and *what* they are for me. I can only find them; I cannot create others that shall exist for me (Husserl, Fifth Cartesian Meditation 1960: 141, emphasis in original).

At least some witnesses might well have had difficulty with the conclusion that they had "created" an Other.

There were a number of positive photo identifications of Essex by civilian and police witnesses. The Narrative, however, presents some as more positive than they appear in the witness interviews. For example, the Narrative says that Hazel Thomas, hotel maid, positively identified a photo of Essex, but in her interview she says the photo she was shown "looks something like [him]" (829). Nonetheless, a strong case is made that some witnesses were certain they saw Essex. Such identification does not, however, eliminate the possibility that a second sniper might also have been seen.

Of the witnesses who were shown photos and asked to identify the person they saw, in addition to those who identified Essex, some said that the person they saw looked similar, some said they could not identify any of the photos, and others selected photos of people other than Essex. Yet others claimed that they saw two people, separately or together, one of whom was Essex. Analysis here is, unfortunately, somewhat difficult because the interviews describing the showing of photos to witnesses identify some photos only by numbers and it is not clear from the context which person is being identified.[8] Nonetheless, photos of five different individuals were tentatively or positively identified by witnesses as the person they saw (one of these photos may have been of Essex):

> #48378 (perhaps a photo of Essex) was said by one witness to look like him but is not (838); by another witness that it looks like him but is not positive (636)
> #48374 identified by one witness (67, 875; interview suggests that the person in the photo had a goatee); another witness said it "looked like him" but also looked like #278255 (816)
> #48376 (Robert Steeward) was identified by one witness (724)
> #163-460 (Curtis J. Moss) was identified by one witness (843)

Police interviewed a number of persons as possible second snipers and, according to the Report, all were eliminated as suspects. It may well be that the police had more grounds for such elimination than is indicated in the Report but did not include it once it had been decided that Essex acted alone. Nonetheless, what is presented in the Report does not seem to eliminate some of these possible second snipers in a definitive way. Without any suggestion of second-guessing the New Orleans Police Department, I offer the following three instances of a possible second sniper that indicate problems for unconstitution given the data available in the Report.

CASE ONE. Carrie Mae Clemmons, hotel maid, said in her interview that she saw the sniper on the 11th floor of Howard Johnson's and he spoke to her. During her interview she was shown photos and asked to identify them:

> A. I ain't seen this man here (pointing to Mark Essex). This man with, the man here had that funny hair and this here (referring to the photograph and B of I number of Robert G. Peters).
> Q. Did you see Robert Peters?
> A. This man (referring to Robert Peters) is the one that came through there with that gun. That's the man I saw.
> Q. Robert Peters is the man you saw on the 11th floor?
> A. I don't know his name, but that's the face, moustache, and everything. This child here (referring to Essex) I've never seen (812).

The definiteness of her identification might make it difficult to refute. Interestingly, the officer who interviewed her stated, without comment but with the potential for dismissing the sighting, that she had been taking 10 gram capsules [sic; 10 milligram pills?] of Valium and sleeping pills (812)—the only interview in which drug use was mentioned.

The person she identified, Robert Gerard Peters, was described by police as being at Charity Hospital on 1/7, at about 10:15 p.m., carrying a pump action shotgun and "had in one of his pockets a particle of red cardboard paper similar to that which is used to wrap an M-80 firecracker.... Under questioning, Peters admitted that he had come to the hospital with the intention of helping police officers. . . .[H]e chose to go there [hospital] since he did know some first aid. He further stated that his mother had told him that she had heard on commercial radio that the police were requesting that anyone with weapons come to the area of the shooting to assist" (264). He was questioned by police and "it was determined that he had not [sic] known connection, either as a principle [sic] or as an accomplice, in the Howard Johnson's shooting incident" (265).

CASE TWO. David F. Moyers, hotel guest, was on the balcony with the sniper (about 60 or 70 feet away). He identified a photo of Robert Steeward, saying, "I feel positive this is the man with the rifle" (724). A Robert Steward was interviewed, but it is not clear whether or not he is the same person. (No mention is made of an interview with a Robert Steeward.) As part of the investigation following the 12/31/72 shooting at Central Lockup, interviews had been conducted with five individuals who were involved in an incident in July 1972. Steward was one of these five; a second was Curtis J. Moss, described in the next case.

CASE THREE. Odissefs Vrettos, an engineer in the Rault Building, who observed the sniper from the 17th floor of the Rault Building overlooking the Howard Johnson's patio, tentatively identified a photo of Curtis J. Moss as similar to one of two snipers he saw but without a moustache and goatee (the second he identified as Essex). Moss was interviewed on January 16, 1973, and "At the time of this interview, it was observed that Moss still had a full goatee. . . ." (276).

The description of interviews with Steward, Moss, and three of their associates concludes: "[T]he investigation into their backgrounds, etc. failed to reveal any possible connection with Mark Essex or the incident at the Howard Johnson's Motel. Their photographs were shown to a number of witnesses to the Howard Johnson's incident, *but they were not identified by anyone* as having been on the scene on January 7, 1973" (278, emphasis added).

Related to sightings of someone other than Essex are sightings of *two* different snipers. Police Officer William Trepagnier "stated that it was his opinion that the negro male sniper at the front of the motel who shot [firefighter] Lt. Ursin was not the same sniper that he had seen at the rear of the motel [Gravier Street side of the 8th floor patio]" (101). The above-mentioned Odissefs Vrettos, looking from the 17th floor of Rault Building towards the patio[9] of Howard Johnson's, described seeing two snipers *together*. He identified Essex (in the morgue) as one of the people he saw and tentatively identified a photo of Curtis J. Moss as similar to the second sniper. Joseph Victor, an employee of the Rault Center and with Vrettos at the time, also identified Essex (in the morgue) and also described a second person. Both described the two they saw as being "together" (285). Although it could be argued that two such sightings confirm one another, the Report offers the following explanation that serves to weaken the evidence:

It should be noted that Vrettos and Victor came into the Criminal Investigation Division Office together, and that it was obvious that they had discussed their observations prior to making their statements. It should further be noted that other witnesses who later positively identified Mark Essex observed Essex about this same time, and noted that he was alone. It should also be noted that there were other persons in the same area, originally thought to be hostages, and it is quite possible that both of these witnesses saw one of these persons. Likewise, many police officers, in uniform and plain clothes, were in the motel at this time, and several of them reported sighting Essex at this time; it is possible that Victor and Vrettos saw one of these police officers (286–7).

The criticism that witnesses had previously discussed their observations was not raised in relation to the three joint interviews with police officers (2 interviews with 2 officers, 1 with 3 officers, see 406, 444, 466). Further reasons to dismiss the contradictory sightings by Vrettos and Victor is indicated by the Report's claim that none of the other witnesses to the patio shooting "observed anyone who might have been construed as being an accomplice of Essex. It is entirely possible that because of the distance involved, and the smoke coming from the motel, that Vrettos was observing a guest of the motel, who might have been near Essex at the time" (285-286).

Particularly problematic for the unconstituting of a second sniper are sightings *after* Essex's death.

Q. [To Police Lt. John M. Lopinto] At about 9:35 PM [on 1/7] a unit identifying itself as Car 850, which are your assigned call numbers, broadcasted the following over Channel 'C,' 'The first guy came out and took a shot at the helicopter and ran back in, he didn't get hit. Then another guy came out on the next pass and fired a few times at the helicopter and then ran out on the roof, and that's the one who's laying out here dead right now on the roof. So there is two different people, and there is definitely another on[e] in there.' Did you personally make this transmission? (486–7).

Lopinto responded no, that Officer Dave Kissee made this transmission. Lopinto stated that he did not see a second subject. No interview with Office Kissee was included in the Report.

At 3:00 a.m. Monday, officers in Car 114 reported sightings of a subject on the roof of Howard Johnson's.

While seated in Car 114, several officers reported hearing rounds being fired to the parking lot on Poydras Street and Loyola Avenue. We then began to check the rooftop of the Howard Johnson's, and we spotted what appeared to be a man on the Poydras Street side of the cubicle facing Loyola Avenue. Officer Barnes directed fire from the Federal Building to this location, but to the best of my recollection, it appeared the shadow or object which was in the corner never moved

> or moved only once. After watching the object remaining stationary, we called for a cease fire at this target (Police Officer Antoine Saacks, 557–8).

Officer Saacks went on to say that he saw this "shadow" with his naked eye but later, using binoculars, saw nothing. His interview suggests that he himself is providing grounds for unconstituting a second sniper.

Describing what he saw from the 14th floor of the Rault Center at approximately 5:00 a.m. on Monday, Sgt. Ronald Macpherson stated:

> the helicopter was ordered to check the roof around the cubicle on the Poydras Street side of the Howard Johnson's building. At this time I was in position at a window and instructed the officers around me not to shoot unless there was a definite target and to be very careful not to hit the cinderblock part of the cubicle because police officers were known to be inside it. While the helicopter was hovering over this cubicle with its lights shining on it, I was observing the cubicle through my rifle scope. At this time I observed an unknown colored male in a white shirt appear briefly from around the outside the cubicle. He looked at the helicopter and then disappeared either into the darkness of the cubicle or into the stairwell. This subject was not in my view long enough for me to react and fire a shot, however, an officer next to me did fire one shot at the subject (498–9).

And, during a 5:00 a.m. Monday helicopter flight over the hotel roof,

> A police officer next to him opened fire, after which Marine Sgt. McLeod, who was by the front side door of the helicopter, yelled that he thought he was hit and that the helicopter was taking fire. The helicopter remained in the area for approximately ten or fifteen seconds before pulling off. During this time, the police officers on board were firing their weapons (Staff Sergeant John H. Payne, USMC, 882).

During the daylight hours of that Monday three officers "responded to several calls of snipers on the Charity Hospital Nurses Home and the La Pavillion and the Veterans Administration Hospital, etc. (all calls were unfounded)" (407). Describing his activities on that day, Detective Ronald Forman stated,

> We responded to numerous calls of sniper incidents in this area [downtown], and checked same out with other officers. After the roof of the Howard Johnson's was secured [i.e., after the assault on Monday afternoon], I and Detective Chetta went to the Howard Johnson's . . .[and] assisted Lt. Roger Bacon in checking out reports of the sniper being seen on the 8th, 9th, and 10th floor area (409).

In the Report there was no other mention of these later sightings.

The many sightings of an increasingly "presumed" rather than "actual" second sniper came in for reinterpretation. One such sighting, for example, was explained in a newspaper story entitled "Waving of 'Mystery Man' on Balcony Cleared Up" (T-P, 1/10/73c). Ed Frashier, hotel guest, said he waved several times from the balcony to let someone know he was there. Thus those who saw Frashier could be said to have seen an Other, a different Other, but not a "sniper Other." Efforts were made to reformulate the "sightings" of a second sniper as sightings of someone "mistakenly" taken to be a sniper, e.g., a police officer, a hotel guest. The Report offers the following explanations for "mistakes":

> [I]t should be noted that while there were varying descriptions given by witnesses and victims of Essex and of his clothes, and the weapon he was carrying, there is no evidence that anyone else participated in or assisted Essex inside the Howard Johnson's Motel. It is a well-known fact, supported by the valued opinions of many skillful investigators and authorities in the field, that witnesses, and more particularly victims to serious crimes, often give varying descriptions of perpetrators and different accounts of what transpired. There is no doubt that the persons involved in the Howard Johnson's incident were under great emotional stress, and particularly those inside the motel were most fearful for their lives. The excitement and fear that they felt undoubtedly incited their imaginations to the extent that the descriptions and accounts they gave were distorted (128).

And some blame for discrepant sightings was attributed to Essex himself, that he *intentionally created the impression* of other snipers. He "wore clothing which was readily removable or reversible, which could have accounted for varying descriptions" (129).

> Mark Essex did enter the motel with the obvious intention to confuse and deceive; his rapid movements throughout the motel, the setting of several fires, and the shootings from different locations all added to the overall confusion which he effectively established (128–9).

> [T]here is no doubt that Essex moved rapidly and deliberately throughout the Howard Johnson's Motel, and that he was able to create an atmosphere of confusion, adding to speculation that more than one subject was inside the motel, causing the turmoil (241).

Thus the initial postulation of a second sniper by police is rendered not only reasonable but a direct consequence of Essex's actions.

Other reasons offered for contradictory sightings related to the conditions at the time:

> Due to the smoke, they [Officers Edward Griffin and Gilbert Johnson] were unable to determine immediately if Essex was a police officer (120).

> Due to the excitement at the time they were on the patio, [Kathleen] McGee [hotel guest] was unable to identify Mark Essex as the negro male that she had seen on the patio with the rifle (96).
>
> He [Thomas W. Holden, USMC, in the helicopter] felt that due to the long hours and the tension, many people were seeing things that were not there (885).

Robert Gustav Stringer, hotel guest, asked for description of the person he saw, gave a few details, then said, "Frankly, when the firing started, I was looking for cover" (708).

Inanimate objects could have been "mistaken" for a sniper. Major Charles A. Wimmler, USMC, in a helicopter that flew over roof, said he never observed a sniper until Essex's death. "[T]he antennas on the elevator building at Howard Johnson's could have been mistaken for being a man especially at night from ground level" (880).

In other cases there was agreement that a person was sighted but confusion over whether or not the person was the sniper. Of a sighting from the roof of the Rault Center around 1:00 p.m. Sunday, Police Officer Edward Griffin said of the person on the roof of Howard Johnson's:

> We were trying to make out or determine whether or not he was a police officer. About that time Gilbert yelled at me, 'It's not a police officer; it looks like he's got a bush comb in his hair.' After Gilbert made this statement, the subject stood up, and we started firing (422).
>
> [In the stairwell near the 3rd floor of Howard Johnson's, shortly after the shooting of the fireman] we saw a man in a suit with a pistol out, and he was running in a stairway, just running in it; and we got down, and they said it was a man with a gun, and I told the policeman that I saw a man with a pistol, and he said that it was probably a detective (Francis Marion Crawford, hotel guest, 654).
>
> Mrs. [Julaine] Gray [observing from the 18th floor the Bank of New Orleans Building at approximately 3:15 p.m. Sunday] advised that while she was watching this man run across the roof she thought he was a policeman, however, there was another individual in another room. . .who she refuses to identify, who told her that he was the sniper and not a policeman (848).

Confusion was also associated with the sighting of "a negro female on the Gravier Street and South Rampart Street side of the patio. . .dressed in a brown sweater and green uniform type dress, and it is believed by this officer she either worked for Howard Johnson's Motel or had obtained a motel uniform and was with the sniper. . . .It was felt by the other officers in the room [8th floor of the Rault Building] from time to time that she was with the sniper, and they and myself would not allow her to accurately point us out, as she continuously looked back towards the two motel rooms and gestured toward us" (Sgt. Donald D. Moore, Sr., 517). The interview with Beatrice Greenhouse, hotel maid, suggests that she was the individual sighted and the Report suggests that her actions could be explained by hysteria rather than association with Essex. Nonetheless, she may at the time have been variously identified as an accomplice, a hostage, or simply as someone caught up in the event.

Given the *assumption* that there was only one sniper, the evidence that sightings at Howard Johnson's were either of Essex or of a police officer, a hotel guest, or some other civilian is certainly plausible. To make such an assumption and tell the story of a single sniper does, however, leave some contradictory sightings unaccounted for, explained away rather than explained. If an assumption had been made that there was a second sniper, some of the sightings might plausibly have been diverted to that story.

Others Are Seeable: Retrospective Sightings

Once Essex was identified and the event reframed to begin on December 31, 1972, the Report identified earlier sightings of "a person" as sightings of Essex–producing what could be termed retrospective sightings. The circumstances of these sightings are quite different from those at Howard Johnson's. Here too fear might have affected perceptions, but the fear was not of a sniper but of someone engaged in a more circumscribed activity: breaking and entering, looking suspicious, shooting a gun (clearly of consequence to the person injured but as an event short-lived), car theft, and a fender-bender. The widespread confusion at Howard Johnson's was absent.

The first such sighting is described as by Reverend Sylvester S. Williams, pastor of First New St. Mark Baptist Church, on 1/1. Williams, however, said that he could not identify any photo–because of poor lighting he couldn't see the face clearly–but the one of Essex looked similar in height and build. The attribution of this sighting to Essex was reinforced by a note left in the church and later deemed to have been written by him. (See below, "Leavings" section.)

The next sightings described in the Report as being of Essex occurred at Joe's Grocery on 1/2. A person with a bloody bandage on his hand entered the grocery store and purchased razor blades and a Schick "Champion" injector razor with a white handle with blue and white stripes. Both Joe Perniciaro, owner, and Darryl Davis, grocery clerk, described the subject in similar terms and both said he had a moustache and goatee and was wearing army fatigue-like clothes. Darryl Davis identified photo #48374, saying, "This is the guy, but his goatee doesn't hang like it does in the picture. It's cut close to the chin" (875). (The Report does not indicate whose photo he identified nor does it state that any photo of Essex showed him with a moustache and/or goatee). After this person left the store, Perniciaro contacted the police, whom he had heard on the radio were looking for someone who was cut or wounded in relation to the shooting at Central Lockup.

A second sighting at Joe's Grocery occurred on 1/7, at 10:30 a.m. A person entered the store, said to Joe, "You come here" (871) or "Come here, you" (877), and shot Perniciaro. A spent shell casing found at the scene was linked to Essex's rifle. According to the Report Narrative, Perniciaro at the time "told the officers that he had been shot because he had talked to the police previously . . . and said the person who shot him was the same one who came to the store on January 2" (65). Interviewed later in the hospital, however, he said that "none of his problems would have happened if he had not gone to the police and that he could not identify the subject who had shot him" (66). Darryl Davis was asked, "Have you ever seen the young man that shot Mr. Perniciaro in or around the grocery before?" (878). He answered "No" but said he thought he could identify him again. Angela Davis, grocery clerk, identified Essex as the gunman.

Some evidence can be used to support the 1/2 and 1/7 sightings as of the same person, namely Essex, and the Report states, "witnesses to the shooting [on 1/7] describing the suspect, give a description closely fitting that of Mark Essex, both in clothing and physical appearance" (149). Interviews with witnesses, however, offer contradictory evidence. Perniciaro's refusal to formally identify the two as the same could be attributed to his decision to avoid involvement with the police, but Darryl Davis' very different descriptions of the two and his statement that they were not the same person are more difficult to dismiss. Witnesses' estimates of height and weight in general may, of course, range widely (as is clear in the Appendix) and thus the discrepancy could be attributed to witnesses' inaccuracies or changes that the sniper himself made. Certainly the person seen on 1/2 might by 1/7 have shaved his beard and goatee, but it improbable that he lost 7 inches and 30 pounds. Angela Davis' claim that the gunman got into a "waiting car" is more problematic and not addressed in the Report. But if Essex was the gunman and had a waiting car, why would he steal one a few minutes later, at 10:37 a.m., when he is described as approaching on foot and stealing Marvin Albert's car?

Albert described the person who stole his car and, although the Report says he positively identified Essex, in the interview he says of photo #48378 (perhaps of Essex but the Report does not say) that it "looks like him, but it is not him" (838). The last sighting prior to those at Howard Johnson's took place at 10:39 a.m. when Tomar Friedman's car was hit by a person she described as a Negro male wearing a white dress shirt. The Report refers to both the Albert and the Friedman sightings as of Essex.

The report thus addresses contradictory sightings in a number of ways. The confusion and danger at the time provide one basis for questioning or dismissing some sightings, especially those at Howard Johnson's. The simple assertion in the Report that a wide range of varying descriptions *are* of Essex to some extent bypasses the problem. Although there may be other grounds not provided in the Report, some of the tentativeness of identifications in the interviews is presented in the Narrative as certainty. Of particular use in dismissing contradictory sightings is the statement that "It is a well-known fact...that witnesses...often give varying descriptions of perpetrators and different accounts of what transpired" (128 and cited above). Witnesses who identified Essex, however, were deemed reliable; it was those who did not who were judged unreliable.

Others and Their Actions Are Hearable

With the large number of armed people on the scene and the number of shots fired, with the acoustics and resulting echoes, as well as the general confusion, it is not surprising that what was heard and what it meant could be subject to retrospective reinterpretation. The Report attributes some of the confusion over sounds to Essex himself, who "carried firecrackers, which when set off, gave the impression that he was in different places" (129).

The sounds of voices may be more compelling evidence than other sounds, but they too are subject to reassignment. Sgt. Donald D. Moore, Sr. who said he saw two snipers, both not Essex, stated:

> After the sniper was cut down on the roof, I definitely heard someone shout in the exact following words, 'Power to the people.' There was no way I could mistake what I heard, and this was heard by numerous persons around me and all of us commented that we just could not understand how anyone could have possibly lived through the barrage which had been shot at the building and in particular the cubicle that day (519).

It is possible, however, to be convinced of *what* one heard but mistaken about *who* said it. Major Charles A. Wimmler, USMC, provided an alternative explanation for the voices heard:

> [O]n January 8, 1973, at approximately 8:00 PM, he was talking with an unidentified police officer, possibly a lieutenant, who stated his men in the Bank of New Orleans Building were yelling down during the night both before and after the one sniper was killed, saying such things as 'Power to the People." He stated the lieutenant told him his men were doing this to try to draw the sniper out; and if there was a second sniper, to draw him into the open. Major Wimmler stated he believes the police officers in the stairwell at Howard Johnson's heard the police officers at the Bank of New Orleans building yelling and mistook the yelling as coming from a second sniper (880–1).

Sounds of gunfire presented particular identification problems. At the time of the event, gunfire suggested danger to those hearing it; its attribution to a sniper provided guidelines for response. Initially, common sense suggested that people who were being shot at were being shot at by the sniper, not by police officers. Once it was determined (during the event) that some of the gunfire came from police, different responses were called for. Hernon describes police shooting from a building across the street into the 16th floor of the hotel, threatening the policemen there. Hernon reports that "in desperation, some men on the sixteenth floor shouted through a broken window [at the police], 'You motherfuckers! Next time we're going to shoot back'" (1978: 233).

> Giarrusso ordered all firing stopped except by marksmen 600 yards off atop the federal building. His order came when policemen on the 17th floor of the hotel said they were being fired on, apparently by their own men (S-I, 1/8/73a).

Gunfire at the same time from different directions or from guns with different sounds initially suggested different snipers.

> [A]t approximately 1:00 PM [Sunday, Heyd] observed what he thought to be rifle fire coming from the 18th floor of the Howard Johnson's, and at the same time observed what he thought to be a lighter caliber weapon firing from the roof of the Howard Johnson's on the Perdido Street side. At this time Fire Fighter Heyd saw neither of the snipers, but stated he felt there were definitely two individuals (Fire Fighter Dennis Heyd, 622–3).

In interviews after the event police officers offered reinterpretations of the meaning of some of the gunfire. Describing the events in the Perdido Street stairwell between the 18th floor and the roof prior to Essex's death, Sgt. Robert Buras stated,

> It was very difficult to distinguish rounds hitting the structure where we were located from rounds that might have been fired from near the structure, that is we couldn't determine from our position if a sniper was nearby on the roof firing at other officers or the noises or reports from the weapons were from the weapons of the officers firing at our position. . . . I also heard reports from what appeared to be a heavy caliber and a light caliber weapon being fired at the same time at the helicopter. I reported by radio to the Command Post the difference in the sounds of the weapons. *I believe now that I could have been hearing the .44 magnum of Essex and at the same time hearing large and small firecrackers going off.* . . . On thinking back on the incident, *I believe that the blasts that appeared to be muzzle flashes coming from the roof door at the top of the stairwell], were actual rounds coming through the steel door being fired by automatic weapons from the marine helicopter with police marksmen* (348–9, emphasis added).

After Essex's death, in the assault on the rooftop Monday afternoon, Sgt. James W. Kavanaugh, Sr., was asked, "[D]id you or your group receive any firing from the boiler room?" He responded, "I could not tell at the time, however, *no one was found in the boiler room so I assume not*" (454, emphasis added). Retrospective analysis thus suggests that one could not have heard firing by a sniper because no sniper was found to have done the firing.

Sounds can stand for an Other and the actions of that Other but by themselves are more ambiguous, more malleable, and less compelling than sightings. Thus they are more amenable to alternative explanations and, after the event, sounds appear to have been easier for witnesses to reassign than sights. Unconstituting a second sniper was facilitated by reassigning some of those sounds to Essex, police, others, or the vagaries of acoustics.

Turn-Taking (Reciprocity)

Some of what was viewed as turn-taking, i.e., *exchanges* of gunfire between police and a sniper, came to be reinterpreted as unintended exchanges between police. Specific instances of police firing on police were recognized at the time of the event, but as isolated instances rather than in relation to one another and as part of a broader picture.

> I heard a call over the porta-mobile they [other police in the room] had with them that there was firing coming from the Rault Center which may be another sniper. At this time I picked up the mike and informed the channel dispatcher that it was the detectives on the 9th floor firing tear gas at the room with the sniper (Sgt. Donald D. Moore, Sr., 518).

Other instances were at the time seen as exchanges between a sniper and police and only later reinterpreted.

> Deputy [David] Munch stated that Essex saw him and fired four or five rounds at his position. The New Orleans Police officers then returned Essex's fire; and during the exchange, Deputy Munch sustained minor gunshot injuries. . . . *It was later learned that Deputy Munch was injured when one of the officers fired a shotgun into a closed window while shooting at Essex. The debris from broken glass and ricocheting shotgun pellets were the causes of Deputy Munch's injuries* (110, emphasis added).

In the following account by Lt. Jake Schnapp, Sr., who participated in helicopter flyovers after Essex's death, reformulation is also included as part of the account.

> At sometime between 3:00 AM and 4:00 AM, on one of the fly-overs by the helicopter, the door opened and *what I thought to be* an exchange of gunfire, between the sniper and my people on that stairwell took place (567, emphasis added).

The Report Narrative offers the following reformulations:

> At about 3:50 AM, January 8, 1973, while the helicopter was flying over the motel near the Perdido Street end of the building, the door to the Perdido Street stairwell, which was propped open by a shotgun

dropped there by Officer Larry Arthur, opened *apparently by the prop wash from the helicopter*. The police officers in the helicopter . . ., *thinking that a second sniper had opened the door*, fired into the stairwell area. The officers in the stairwell. . ., *thinking that they were receiving fire from another sniper*, returned fire through the stairwell door. During the encounter, Sgt. O'Sullivan sustained an injured left ear; Sgt. Buras sustained injuries to this left shoulder; and Officer Galjour sustained injuries to his head and neck; and Officer Siegel received an injury to his eye. *These injuries are believed to have been caused by cement splinters knocked loose from the wall of the stairwell by the bullets fired from the helicopter, or by bullet fragments.* Also during this brief encounter, the helicopter was struck three times by bullets fired from the stairwell (125–6, emphasis added; see also 40–41).

The roof assault on Monday afternoon was also formulated at the time as an exchange between police on the roof and the sniper in the bunker. Detective Lawrence J. Delsa reported, "we heard someone cry out, 'He's shooting back through the door'" (385). "Several officers were injured by ricocheting bullets, *but at this time there was no way to know whether it was ricocheting bullets or firing by the sniper from that building*" (Lt. Jake Schnapp, Sr., 568, emphasis added).

Only in the aftermath of the event, when witness reports were seen in the light of one another and the assumption of a second sniper was taken to be problematic, did it begin to seem plausible that many of the exchanges, especially those after Essex's death, might be attributed to police. Some police were said to have been hit by ricochets rather than being shot at directly, others to have been accidentally hit, e.g., by helicopter fire–the "accident" not that people were shot, for shots were aimed at them, but that they were police officers, "mistakenly shot," and not a sniper. "In retrospect, it appeared the squad and the men in the helicopter had been firing at each other" (S-I, 1/15/73, byline John Kifner, *New York Times*).

At the time of the event, the absence of centralized police communication and the presence of unauthorized or misdirected shooting tended to obscure the possibility that police might have been shooting at one another. A space was thereby left to be inhabited by a second sniper. Retrospective reattribution of the shooting either to Essex or to the police reformulated turn-taking as occurring between Essex and police or police and police. The second sniper's "turn" was rendered irrelevant and the space available to be inhabited by that second sniper contracted. Nonetheless, without direct evidence linking *all* ammunition and spent shells found in and around Howard Johnson's to Essex or police—a seemingly impossible task given the amount of shooting that occurred—the claim that all the shooting was done either by Essex or the police of necessity remains speculative.

Leavings

Items found by police and linked (or linkable) to Essex served as evidence to plot a path for him beginning on December 31, 1972 at Central Lockup and through the Perdido Street vacant lots to the Oliver Van Horn Company, the Burkart Manufacturing Company, The First New St. Mark Baptist Church, Joe's Grocery, a second visit to The First New St. Mark Baptist Church, a second visit to Joe's Grocery, and, on 1/7, to and through Howard Johnson's. Some leavings were directly linked to Essex (e.g., spent shell casings linked to the rifle confirmed as sold to Essex and found by his body). Leavings, of course, do not say *who* left them; such determinations are inferential. That leavings can be attributed to Essex does not prove that he was the leaver or that a second person was not responsible for some of those leavings. Nonetheless a plausible path for Essex can be constructed from leavings, supplemented by sightings of a person retrospectively taken to be Essex.

The determination that the event "began" at Central Lockup was in part established by the identification of .44 caliber spent shell casings found at the scene (and one bullet removed from the body of Officer Hosli) which laboratory tests determined had been fired by the rifle found by Essex's body. The beginning of the path from Central Lockup to the Burkart Manufacturing Company is described as follows:

> A total of seven shots were fired into the Lockup [on 12/31/72]. The sniper then fled across the railroad tracks and the I-10 Expressway, dropping some of his equipment as he fled, leaving boot prints in the soft mud along both shoulders of the expressway, and through the 900 block of South Dupre Street, where he dropped more equipment, and finally through the 4100 block of Euphrosine Street, and into a warehouse at 1065 South Gayoso Street [Burkart Manufacturing Company] (48–49).

A Colt .38 caliber blue steel revolver containing six live .38 caliber rounds was found in an open lot at the rear of Central Lockup. The serial number of the revolver had been filed off, fingerprints on it were not identified, and no evidence was discovered that Essex had purchased or used it. In the same place a string of 180 unspent firecrackers was found. In addition to these items and to spent shell casings found along the route (some of which were linked to the rifle found by Essex's body) were a number of other leavings deemed relevant to police in plotting this part of the path, including footprints (according to the laboratory report consistent with the boots found on Essex's body); a brown leather bag containing three cans of lighter fluid, a 65-foot roll of wire (that laboratory tests determined was identical to the wire attached to the red, black, and green revolutionary flag found at Howard Johnson's and to the coil of wire later found in Essex's apartment); strings of unspent firecrackers; a gas mask; and, inside the Burkart Manufacturing Company, another brown leather bag identical to the one found earlier along the path, a flashlight (with unknown fingerprints), a gas mask canister (prints not identified as Essex's until after 1/8), a pair of blue and green cloth work gloves, a man's tan long sleeve corduroy shirt, and live rounds of .38 caliber ammunition,

The first sighting of a person taken to be Essex as he followed the path postulated by police—although he was only so identified *after* the event at Howard Johnson's—occurred on January 1 at 6:30 p.m. at The First New St. Mark Baptist Church. Police responded to a report of a prowler by the pastor of the church, Rev. Sylvester S. Williams, but by the time the police arrived the prowler had disappeared. Police returned to the church on January 3 after a report of a person hiding inside the church. No such person was found, but police did find a cloth tied with wire and containing .38 live rounds and a handwritten note that began, "Dear Pastor, I am sorry for breaking the lock on your church door but pastor at 2:00 I felt I had to get right with the Lord. . . " (290). The note was later identified as being in Essex's handwriting (148, 184).

The second sighting of a person claimed by police to be Essex (although witnesses offered contradictory descriptions and claims) took place on January 2 at 6:00 p.m. A Negro male with a bloody bandage on his hand entered the Joe's Grocery and purchased razor blades and a Schick "Champion" injector razor with a white handle with blue and white stripes. A Schick razor later found in Room 808 of Howard Johnson's was said to be similar to the one purchased.

There is then a gap in the path that extends to Sunday, January 7, at 10:30 a.m.

The Police Report of the events prior to January 7 can be read as if Essex alone left a trail from Central Lockup to Joe's Grocery, a trail to be followed by the police. The leavings were used by the police to isolate the event both in time (December 31–January 7) and in space. Thus the event "began" at Central Lockup and "ended" with Essex's death. The second sniper and attributions made to that sniper were rendered unnecessary—tangential if not irrelevant. That these leavings *could* be linked to Essex strengthened the view that he acted alone. Some of these leavings could have been attributed to a second sniper (e.g., those with unidentified fingerprints or with none), but in the absence of any clear evidence pointing to the presence of a second sniper, they were not.

How and why Essex might have left such a trail is unclear. The leavings could certainly be read as suggesting that Essex had prepared himself with a variety of equipment; they could also be read as his being panicked, disorganized, unwilling or unable to hide his tracks, sloppy, or not particularly skillful—neither hiding his tracks nor holding onto his equipment.

On January 8, the situation at Howard Johnson's was deemed secure and police searched the hotel for evidence. Sightings on January 7 of a sniper on the 8th, 9th, 10th, 11th, and 18th floors and the roof may have guided the search. Leavings were used to plot a path for Essex through the hotel. Relevant to the process were the locations of dead bodies and the bullets removed from them; evidence of fires set (on four floors); firecrackers; and spent shell casings identified as belonging to Essex's rifle. Some leavings pointed directly to Essex; others could not be so attributed because of their ambiguity (e.g., damaged bullets). Of the bullets removed from those injured or killed, five (including one from the grocer, Joe Perniciaro, earlier in the day) were determined by laboratory examination to be from Essex's gun; one bullet removed was too damaged to be identified; the Report provides no information about other bullets that killed or injured victims. Shell casings found throughout the hotel were linked to Essex's rifle.

To suggest the amount of ammunition left behind in and around the hotel, a single police officer shooting from the 14th floor of the Bank of New Orleans Building onto the roof of Howard Johnson's said, "I would estimate that during this period of time I fired through the 30-06 rifle about 400 rounds of ammunition. About 350 of these rounds were used to make a hole in the 12" section of the concrete wall" (Det. John Dupre, 396). Given the enormous amount of ammunition, spent and unspent, found after the event, it would have been impossible to link all of it to specific people—Essex, a second sniper, police, or others. Nonetheless, no found ammunition was described as clearly pointing to a second sniper.

Seven people in or observing Howard Johnson's and one witness earlier in the day described a person (sniper) wearing a blue jacket. (Contradictory evidence was provided by seven other witnesses, who described the person they saw as wearing an army-like or camouflage-like fatigue jacket; two others a green jumpsuit; two others a leather jacket.) Evidence attributed to Essex included "Essex's blue quilted jacket and Schick injector razor found on chair in Room 808 [of Howard Johnson's]; jacket later identified as having been worn by Essex, and the razor has having been purchased by Essex at Joe's Grocery" (photo caption, n.p.). The finding of the blue jacket and its attribution to Essex could resolve some of the discrepant descriptions of clothing—some might have seen him before he removed the jacket, others after. Two witnesses at Joe's Grocery and two in the hotel described the sniper as having an item that resembled the red, black, and green flag recovered on the 18th floor of Howard Johnson's.

What counts as a relevant leaving is, of course, a judgment. Any search for the leavings of one or more snipers could have been compromised both by the number of police and amount of equipment in the hotel and by the fact that a number of guests who evacuated the hotel left their belongings behind and were only allowed to return for them after the search. Sorting though leavings in an 18-floor hotel that had been under siege for a day was obviously a complex task. Leavings that could be attributed to Essex might have been guided by sightings; there were few if any guidelines for identifying leavings of an unidentified second sniper. Leavings may tell many stories—the story of Essex is but one—and they may be especially difficult to read when there is no identified or at least clearly postulated specific other to whom they might be assigned.

Speculation and Conspiracy Theories

Postulating the existence of a broad conspiracy or a second sniper is dependent in part upon the consequences of doing so or failing to do so. Initially such postulations served to make sense of a variety of events, address public safety concerns, and provide access to federal aid. The eventual conclusion that there had been no broad conspiracy and no second sniper had very practical value: the event was over, the public safe.

No evidence of a broad conspiracy was discovered. A number of people were considered possible co-conspirators either before or during the event. In addition to the three people identified by witnesses but cleared by police (Robert Gerard Peters, Curtis J. Moss, and Robert Steeward/Steward; see above, "Sightings"), Rodney Frank, a friend of Essex's from the Army and with whom he had maintained contact, was considered and interviewed. "To what degree Rodney Frank influenced Essex will never be known; it is known, however, that Frank is a devout Muslim and anti-white" (242). Frank's interview states "that on Sunday, January 7, 1973. . .he spent the entire day in the [Muslim] temple" (272). The interview concludes, "[T]here was no evidence uncovered which would indicate that Frank participated in Essex's activities between December 31, 1972 and January 7, 1973" (273).

There is, however, speculation that Frank may have been involved prior to the event.

> [I]t is estimated that Essex probably fired in excess of 100 rounds but apparently less than 150 rounds, which would indicate that he had previously acquired three (3) boxes of ammunition. . . . Coincidentally,. . .three (3) boxes, or 150 rounds of similar ammunition were reported missing from the sporting goods department of Schwegmann's Super Market. . . .A box of fifty (50) Winchester Western .38 caliber 200 grain police special ammunition [designed for use in a pistol] was found on the scene of the Central Lockup shooting; this box was marked 'Schwegmann's'. . .(251–2).

Rodney Frank had worked at Schwegmann's, but the conclusion that he assisted Essex in stealing ammunition is at best tenuous.

In describing possible co-conspirators, the Report concludes:

> [S]everal names of individuals were mentioned by sources of information as possibly having some connection with these incidents. . . but in the final analysis, each of these individuals were eliminated as potential suspects in some type of conspiracy. It should be noted that throughout these investigations, the investigating officers uncovered a number of rumors and allegations, which simply could not be proved with any factual evidence. . .(5).

For the most part, speculation and conspiracy theories were replaced with evidence taken to support the claim that Essex acted alone and not as part of a conspiracy. The absence of direct evidence of either a conspiracy or a second sniper reinforced that claim.

The Report does not provide detailed grounds for eliminating the above-mentioned or other possible co-conspirators. Given the conclusion of the Report that Essex acted alone, it is not surprising that extensive information about a now-unconstituted second sniper was not included, but, for the purposes of phenomenological analysis, further information would have been useful. Were contradictory sightings fully considered? Were explanations and alibis of possible co-conspirators thoroughly investigated? Were some initially unidentified fingerprints later identified? It may well be so, but the Report does not say. Any space left for a second sniper may be in part epiphenomenal, attributable to lacunae in the Report itself. Nonetheless, the absence of phenomenologically relevant information provides a space for a second sniper—a small space, perhaps only a theoretical space, perhaps an implausible space, but a space nonetheless.

LINGERING TRACES OF A SECOND SNIPER

> [T]o the idea of the real...itself, and to the idea as a pure form, there belongs correlatively an infinite system of experiences which set up a system of pure harmony (*through the continued exclusion of what is experienced as discrepant and the adoption of what agrees*) and which characterize themselves as...experiences (Husserl, before 1928: 305, emphasis added).

But what was experienced as discrepant could not be altogether excluded. Harmony remains compromised.

Given the absence of incontrovertible evidence, i.e., a body of a second sniper, either alive or dead, the possibility though unlikelihood of a second sniper was maintained in final police reports, serving to justify the initial supposition of two snipers as reasonable, albeit either mistaken or unverifiable.

> There has been no evidence uncovered which would indicate that anyone else was involved at any time. No witnesses have been found whose statements could positively implicate a second party; the statements of those who seem to implicate someone else have either been disproved by physical evidence or by other, more reliable witnesses, or *nothing could be found to substantiate their statements* (6, emphasis added).

Nonetheless, the existence of a second sniper continued to remain a possibility for some witnesses. On the 25th anniversary of the event, 1/7/98, *The Times-Picayune* published a retrospective by Dennis Persica that stated, "there are some who still maintain he had accomplices":

> Though Krinke[10] thinks the reported sightings of other snipers were erroneous, he doesn't buy the one-sniper theory. "I believe there was more than one, and that one of them got out in the chaos of removing

the guests from the building," Krinke said. "He slipped in with that and made his way out." [Police Officer William] Trepagnier agrees: "My gut feeling is, I shot at two different people" (T-P, 1/7/98).

A December 14, 2002 retrospective entitled "30 year anniversary of NOLA sniper" states, "veterans of the Howard Johnson's siege remain certain Essex did not act alone" (http://tchouptrack.blogspot.com/2004/09/30-year-anniversary-of-nola-sniper.html). And the website for the New Orleans *Gambit* (http://bestof neworleans.com/gyrobase/Content?oid =oid%3A29448) in a story on January 7, 2003 entitled "The Heroes of Howard Johnson's" states that "the issue [of a second sniper] continues to divide active and former NOPD officers" (byline Allen Johnson, Jr.).

What particular evidence compromises harmoniousness? What sightings, leavings and activities might be assigned to a second sniper? Identifying Essex as the only sniper and attributing as much evidence as possible to him leaves a rather constricted and odd space for a second sniper to inhabit, but a space nonetheless. Were a second sniper assumed to exist, some of what was attributed to Essex could be reassigned. In what follows, however, I consider only those possible traces not already assigned to Essex.

Contradictory sightings provide one space for a second sniper, for witnesses offered conflicting descriptions, denied that the person they saw was Essex, identified photos of others, could not identify photos of Essex, said they saw two snipers together or, on separate occasions, saw two different snipers. Many explanations can be offered for such discrepancies. Terms used in descriptions, for example, are relative: the sniper's hair was variously described as a short, a medium, and a large bush–the criteria for judgment are not offered. Similarly, the sniper was described as a Negro with light, medium, and dark skin. Size estimates as well are relative. Essex was said to be 5'7"; some witnesses described the sniper as 5' to 5'3" (although one witness who said 4'11" to 5' positively identified Essex), others as 5'10" and above. The identification of a person with a moustache and/or goatee remains unclarified. Witness error was used to account for some discrepancies. Although witness error may be "well-known," the Report only invokes it when someone other than Essex is identified. Certainly one explanation for the discrepancies in descriptions is that there was a second sniper.

On January 7, prior to the event at Howard Johnson's, Angela Davis, cashier, describing the shooting at Joe's Grocery, said, "[T]he young man fired the rifle and shot once at Joseph Perniciaro, then fled down Gayoso Street to Thalia Street *where there was a car waiting for him.* My brother, Darryl Davis, saw him get in a car" (871, emphasis added). In Darryl Davis' interview, however, he simply says that outside the store "I lost sight of him, but I saw something go by quick on Thalia Street heading towards Broad Street crossing Dupre Street" (878). These two sightings could certainly be dismissed on a variety of grounds–confusion, mistaken perception, etc. If, however, an assumption were made that there had been a second sniper, such evidence might have been used to construct a path for that second sniper.

Another anomalous sighting, which the police could not confirm, was provided by Robert Joe Reynolds, who

> related that at about 8:30 AM, January 7, 1973, he was standing on the sidewalk in front of the Howard Johnson's Motel, at which time he saw two negro male subjects with three suitcases and a large paper bag. He approached these two subjects and asked them if they could spare some money, and one of the subjects offered to pay him a dollar if he would carry his luggage into the motel. Reynolds stated that he carried two of the suitcases and was accompanied by the subject who offered him the money, while the other subject stayed outside with the other suitcase and paper bag. He returned outside and got the other suitcase and the paper bag and brought them to the room where he had previously brought the other suitcases. When he reached the room carrying the paper bag, he turned it over and several boxes fell onto the floor. He stated that he believed that these boxes contained bullets. . . . *It should be noted that Reynolds is illiterate and could not read any writing on the boxes, if there was a*ny. . . . Reynolds described the subject who accompanied him to the room and paid him the dollar as being a negro male, 5 feet 8 inches tall, 135 to 140 pounds, dark brown complexion, slender build, short black hair, and wearing black rimmed sunglasses; he could give no description of the second subject (280–1, emphasis added).

Reynolds' illiteracy can serve to weaken the evidence he offers and the Report concludes, "There is no other information to substantiate Reynolds' story and nothing to indicate that the boxes he saw contained bullets" (281). Since the first sighting on 1/7/73 of a person claimed to be Essex was not until 10:30 a.m. (at Joe's Grocery), timing makes it possible for him to have been one of the two described by Reynolds. The Report does not indicate that any unidentified suitcases were found, but neither does it state that all suitcases left behind were identified and reclaimed or returned.

Despite statements made by police that the escape of a second sniper would have been difficult, unguarded stairwells (as well as the elevator shaft) might have provided an escape route. The evacuation of guests and the large number of police on the scene, including those in plainclothes, of necessity produced a certain amount of confusion. The presence of police officers who were black could have served as cover for the escape of a second sniper who was black. This issue was addressed in some of the interviews. One was conducted with William F. Downs, hotel guest, by members of the Houston Police Department on 1/26/73. Downs said he left room 929 of the hotel because of fire and went to the lobby (he estimated the time as 9:45 a.m., an hour earlier than the timeline offered in the Report):

> Q. Did you see an armed black male?

A. No.
Q. Did you see any colored people at the time?
A. I saw several of them, but as far as I know they were colored officers. There were about seventy-five or eighty officers there that did not have uniforms on.
Q. The black officers, you did see black people with guns without uniforms?
A. Yes.
Q. What gave you the impression they were officers?
A. They were mingling with the other officers; most of them had badges pinned to their shirts or something.
Q. Did you see any that didn't have badges?
A. Not that I recall.
Q. How were they dressed?
A. Various dress, khakis, street clothes.
Q. Are there any of these black people with guns that stick out in your mind more than others?
A. No, not really (695).

And, in an interview conducted with Robert J. Stephens, hotel guest, by the Phoenix Police Department, Phoenix, Arizona, 1/23/73:

Q. Did you see an armed black male; if so, where and at what time? Please describe in detail.
A. I saw a group of blacks at a table in the coffee shop. They did not appear to be armed. I saw armed black plainclothes men from the police department (761).

That police officers did not necessarily know the others with whom they were working could have provided anonymity for a second sniper.

Certainly the escape routes were not covered at all times.

> I made periodic checks of the exits in the garage. Upon checking the positions around 10:30 PM [Sunday evening], it was discovered that some positions were not manned and that the people that were in these positions had gone to the 18th floor once it was learned that there was only one sniper (this was the word that got out) (Lt. Peter Hand, 429).

Escape might also be suggested by the following statement by Robert J. Stephens, hotel guest, but the Report offers no clarification of this event:

> About 1:30 PM [Sunday] I was standing with a group of officers two blocks west of the motel on the southeast corner. I saw a black 1965-66 Chevrolet going west very fast, coming from the area of the motel. There was an unmarked police unit in pursuit about two blocks behind the old Chevrolet and a marked unit behind the unmarked unit. One of the policemen on the corner where I was jumped into his

marked unit and followed. I watched until they were out of sight. Shortly, the second marked unit returned. I never learned what the chase was about (762).

If the sightings of a sniper after Essex's death are taken as legitimate, the escape of a second sniper would indeed have to be postulated.

Against this background, and working with discrepancies in witnesses' statements as well as gaps in the Report–gaps that the police may have filled but simply did not include in the Report–I suggest the following path for a second sniper. I am neither criticizing nor second-guessing the police investigation, nor am I taking a stand on whether or not there was indeed a second sniper.[11] My focus is only on what could be seen as left over after assigning as much as possible of the available evidence to Essex.

A PATH FOR A SECOND SNIPER

At Central Lockup, a second sniper might have brought the Colt revolver—but didn't use it and left it behind (the unidentified fingerprints could belong to him). His role might have to carry equipment; if so, however, he seems to done a rather poor job, given what was left along the way. Unless Essex's footprints were the only ones found along the path from Central Lockup to First New St. Mark Baptist Church, other footprints could belong to a second sniper (but without shoes or boots to match, such footprints would not be assignable and might well have gone unnoticed). No mention is made in the Report of unidentified footprints.

A second sniper might have gone alone to Joe's Grocery on 1/2. Darryl Davis, grocery clerk, said that person he saw that day was not the one who shot the grocer on 1/7 and Angela Davis, who does not seem to have been present on 1/2, identified the 1/7 shooter as Essex. Perniciaro initially said both sightings were of the same person but then retracted his claim. One reason offered for the retraction was his fear of retaliation, but he could, upon reflection, have decided that his initial identification had been wrong. No evidence is provided for how the shooter might have learned of Perniciaro's visit to the police.

A second sniper might have gone to Howard Johnson's at 8:30 a.m. on Sunday, January 7 (with Essex?) to leave ammunition in a hotel room and later waited in a car for Essex while he shot the grocer.

There is relatively strong evidence given by police responding to the scenes that Pernirciaro at Joe's Grocery was shot at 10:30 a.m., the theft of Albert's car occurred at 10:37, and the hit and run at 10:39. Some witnesses at the hotel, however, claimed that the first events inside the hotel began at 10:30 a.m. or even earlier. Certainly these witnesses could have misestimated time, but, if they did not, the timing suggests a second sniper whose task was to gain access to hotel floors and perhaps begin setting fires.

These time discrepancies might be used to plot the path of a second sniper inside Howard Johnson's, especially before 10:45 a.m., the time at which, according to police estimates, Essex arrived at the hotel parking garage in Albert's stolen car. Some of these time discrepancies were associated with sightings inside Howard Johnson's of a person significantly different from Essex and that could have been a second sniper. Prior to sightings on the patio, some witnesses who saw a sniper on the 8th, 9th, 18th, and 11th floors said that he looked similar to the photo of Essex, some identified photos of another person, and some were not able to identify any photos. Although it may be unlikely, it does not seem impossible, given the evidence, that some witnesses, especially those who estimated the time of sighting as before Essex's postulated arrival at 10:45, saw a sniper other than Essex. Indeed, some of those who identified Essex might have been in error.

During the time of the patio shootings (10:57 a.m. to 12:10 p.m.), a few witnesses described seeing two different people (at separate times). Two witnesses described a sniper in a hotel room around noon on Sunday at a time when another sniper was reported to have been seen on the patio. Others described seeing a sniper on one floor while fire broke out on another floor. A second sniper, rather than Essex, might have lit fires and set off firecrackers.

Unidentified ammunition at Howard Johnson's might be used to plot a second sniper's path, but the amount of ammunition fired by police (both police-issued and personal) and police exchanging weapons with one another made identification of all the ammunition an impossible task, especially without a weapon for comparison. Estimates of police on the scene run as high as 700, and, although not all fired their weapons, certainly an enormous number of spent shells was left behind.

Some witnesses reported seeing a rifle or a shotgun, some just a shotgun; Essex was found with a rifle. Some claimed the gun they saw had a scope, others that it did not. Police Officer William Trepagnier stated that at both times when he saw a sniper, the weapon appeared to be equipped with a scope (101). A newspaper account states that Essex's "weapon was equipped with a standard sight—no telescopic sight. . . " (S-I, 1/10/73b, byline Lanny Thomas). The Report does not mention whether or not Essex's rifle had a scope, but presumably either it did or didn't. Witnesses could certainly be unfamiliar with firearms, making such identification uncertain, though some witnesses seemed quite knowledgeable, even identifying photos of the weapon they saw. Robert C. Beamish, hotel guest, was shown photos of guns, including a Ruger .44 magnum carbine rifle (the gun found by Essex's body). He stated, "None of these photos seems to be the type of weapon used" (646). A second sniper could have had a shotgun and/or a rifle with a scope.

Some fingerprints were found that were not identified and thus could have been left by a second sniper. Some of those interviewed as possible second snipers had previous police records; presumably their prints were on file and checked, though the Report does not say. Whatever the reason, some fingerprints remain unexplained.

Had a second sniper been on the scene, some or all of the sightings after Essex's death could be explained. Those include sightings of a sniper on the hotel roof between 9:45 p.m. on Sunday and 5:00 a.m. on Monday; the presumed person in the rooftop bunker at 2:00 on Monday when police stormed it; the sighting of a person in the air conditioning ducts; and continued reports on Monday of sightings within the hotel. The second sniper might then have escaped through unguarded routes or openly by passing as a police officer, hotel guest, or employee.

Did a second sniper leave no traces or were such traces overlooked or assigned to Essex? Was a second sniper skilled or simply lucky? What specific activities might be assigned to him during the event? Or did he never exist? That Essex was responsible for much of what happened seems certain, the evidence compelling. Ultimately, however, the existence of this second sniper, this Other, remains uncertain–unlikely, perhaps, but not impossible.

NOTES

1. "Gurrusso" would seem to refer to Police Supt. Clarence B. Giarrusso; The Police Report provides no further information about the "two innocent [sic] brothers."

2. See Chapter 1, footnote 9 for a description of the contents of the report.

3. Although the shooting at Howard Johnson's did not occur until January 7, 1973, the scope of the event was expanded to include what were determined to be related events, a point elaborated below.

4. Here as elsewhere in interviews with police, there is a possibility that the officers engaged in some reconstruction of memories in light of the official movement towards the idea of there never having been a second sniper.

5. For a time an earlier starting point was considered: the October 29, 1972 arson fire in the Rault Building (within sight of Howard Johnson's) which killed seven people and for which no arrests were made. After the Howard Johnson's event, the fire was reinvestigated but no evidence was found to suggest that it was related.

6. [Corrected] refers to Carr's emendation of Husserl's statement in his English translation.

7. See Appendix for details of sightings.

8. Follow-up with the New Orleans Police Department was impossible since many records were lost in Hurricane Katrina. The Report itself had been lost and was only available in the New Orleans Public Library.

9. Both Vrettos and Victor said they were looking at the 10th floor; the patio was on the 8th floor. Their description, however, suggests that they were looking at the patio.

10. The article does not identify him further. August Krinke is listed in the Report as one of the police officers present, but no interview with him is included.

11. My goal has not been to argue for the existence of a second sniper but to explore the constitution and unconstitution of that sniper. Nonetheless, I have been asked on a number of occasions what I personally think: Was there a second sniper? I embarked on this study suspending both belief and doubt. At the conclusion of the study, I remain suspended.

CHAPTER 5.
CONCLUSION

What, then, is an Other made of? Out of what elements in any specific situation is an Other constituted? I began Chapter 2 by proposing the following:

> Prior assumptions and expectations create a space for the Other. Immediate concerns and needs outline that space. The space thus created is filled in with common-sense ideas about what an Other is and is not capable of and with sights, sounds, and indications of turn-taking. These are linked by common-sense theories and speculation, all to some extent constrained by the outline. New or reformulated assumptions and evidence, however, can change the meaning of the constituent elements or change the very outline itself. When expectations change, when the *existence* of an Other is denied, the same evidence can, though with varying degrees of difficulty, be reinterpreted to support the *nonexistence* of that Other. In that process, both the evidence and those who provide it can come in for reassessment and reevaluation.

Throughout the foregoing I have offered support for these general claims with data drawn from the Case of the New Orleans Sniper. I now suggest the following specific features relevant to the constitution of an Other. Such features may be relevant not only when the Other is problematic but also when the Other is unproblematic–for any Other is potentially open to challenge as an Other. I include brief excerpts from the sniper data (some previously cited) as illustrative reminders.

The existence of an Other is plausible.[1] Initially there was no reason not to believe that there at least *could be* a second sniper. John Tobin, hotel guest, said, "It didn't seem possible that one man could run that fast and start those fires" (T-P, 1/12/73, byline John McMillan). Trial runs conducted by police after the event, however, demonstrated that it was indeed possible for one person to have done so. Nonetheless, the existence of a second person was not refuted by that demonstration–a second Other remained plausible, though perhaps somewhat less so. Plausibility is a starting point but not necessarily sufficient to confirm the existence of another (here the second sniper). Further confirmation of that Other can be provided by descriptions of people sighted who are significantly different from one another, sounds of more than one person, the determination that more is done than one person can do, and what one person can leave behind. Faced with conflicting evidence, the postulation of a second person—or some other explanation—is required.

A person is a kinetic/tactile-kinesthetic body. (See Sheets-Johnstone, e.g., 1996, 2003.) A person as well as parts of a person are visible, audible, and capable of movement; these signs can serve as evidence of an Other. Ed Frashier, hotel guest, said that he saw two men fighting in the hallway, then "a man's arm protruding from a door with a rifle in it," (S-I, 1/9/73c). Evidence, however, can be problematic in a number of ways. Major Charles A. Wimmler, USMC, for example, suggested, "[T]he antennas on the elevator building at Howard Johnson's could have been mistaken for being a man especially at night from ground level" (PR: 880). Hearing a person has its own ambiguity, especially when *who* is speaking (e.g., a sniper or police) is based solely on auditory evidence. Detective Lawrence J. Delsa, describing what he heard from the hotel stairwell after Essex was killed, said, "We could hear voices, but they were not as distinct as the voice we heard from the sniper that was killed, and we could not really determine if they were on the roof or not" (PR: 385–6). The claim that one has seen and/or heard a person may be undermined by later evidence. Attributions to two bodies may be reassigned to one body or otherwise explained away. Signs of a kinetic/tactile-kinesthetic body may be reformulated to be signs of something else. Only in the absence of problems are such signs strongly evidentiary.

Indications of present or past action can stand for the existence of an Other. Actions can stand for a person, but they may also be otherwise explained. Attributing actions to a specific actor involves inferences that, although plausible at the time, may be refuted retrospectively. Some of the police officers "shot at" by the sniper were later said to have been "shot at" by ricochets or by other officers. The initial claim that a sniper opened the stairwell door prior to shooting at the helicopter was later reformulated as the door having been blown open by the draft from the helicopter. What are initially seen as actions may be reassigned to other people or to no one–taken to be simply the workings of the physical world.

A person is subject to physical laws, however those laws are formulated. "[Fire Superintendent] San Salvador said he saw two gunflashes from the hotel at the same instant while the sniping was going on. 'One gunman can't make two muzzle flashes that way'" (S-I, 1/16/73a). Being in two places at once violates physical laws. If evidence suggests that physical laws would be violated, and if those laws are taken to be inviolable, then claims regarding the existence of an Other may be reworked in compliance with those laws. Setting slow-starting fires and setting off firecrackers made it possible, for example, to address a sniper's being in two places at once: the sniper was in two places but at two different times. The escape of a second sniper initially challenged physical laws–there was no escape route. David Huber, a police sharpshooter, stated,

"There's no way he (a second sniper) could have gotten off the roof. All three exits were blocked and the 18th floor was completely sealed off" (S-I, 1/9/73, byline Angus Lind). Later evidence challenging this claim made it possible for a person to escape without violating physical laws–though "It would take a very cool operator indeed to walk past police—which he would have had to do—after having been in a combat situation for at least 10 hours or more" (S-I, 1/12/73, byline Allan Katz). Attention thus turned to social rather than physical possibilities.

A person is subject to common-sense rules, notably here "acting like a person" as well as "acting like a sniper." Before Essex was killed, "the sniper was on the roof calling out 'Happy New Year, F–k the pigs, Come on up M—r F—r, I want three more'" (James W. Kavanaugh, Sr., 454). In this respect, the sniper could be said to have been acting like a sniper, such words reasonably attributable to him. Who else would utter them? Only in retrospect were some such statements attributed to police–acting "like police" by trying to lure the sniper into the open. One possible explanation for an escape by a second sniper is that he could have acted not like a sniper but like a police officer or hotel guest. One who acts like another kind of person, i.e., not a sniper, has resources for escape. (One who does not act like a person, e.g., a mannequin, can be redefined as not a person at all.) Common sense serves as a general framework for identifying an Other–an Other is someone who acts like an Other, and, if relevant, a specific kind of Other.

Construction of an Other takes place in social settings. Claims of an Other's existence may be either confirmed or denied by others present or by later analysts. The postulated reliability of those who claim (or deny) the existence of an Other becomes consequential, as do the conditions under which those claims were made–stress, limited visibility, confusing circumstances, danger. Claims may be presented along with social confirmation to forestall attributions of unreliability. Regarding a sighting after Essex's death, Sgt. Ronald Macpherson stated, "This subject was not in my view long enough for me to react and fire a shot, however, an officer next to me did fire one shot at the subject" (PR: 499). Those who maintain the existence of an Other (a second sniper) in the face of official evidence to the contrary may find social situations compromised, e.g., "the issue [of a second sniper] continues to divide active and former NOPD officers." (http://bestofneworleans.com/gyrobase/Content?oid= oid%3A29448, 1/7/03, byline Allen Johnson, Jr.). Social settings are thus relevant for the constitution of an Other as well as for sustaining or unconstituting that Other, with important implications for the participants in those settings.

The existence of a given Other is thus necessarily relative and tentative, subject to later confirmation or refutation.

> [T]he world is never given to the subject and the communities of
> subjects in any other way than as the subjectively relative valid world
> with particular experiential content and as a world which, in and
> through subjectivity, takes on ever new transformations of meaning;
> and that even the apodictically persisting conviction of one and the
> same world, exhibiting itself subjectively in changing ways, is a con-
> viction motivated purely within subjectivity, a conviction whose
> sense—the world itself, the actually existing world—never surpasses
> the subjectivity that brings it about (Husserl, n.d.: 337).

Whether or not the Other in general is given in experience, a specific Other is not necessarily so given. My findings raise questions about givenness by exploring ways that the Other can be constituted rather than directly grasped. To speak of "grasping" the Other is especially inadequate when it is not clear whether or not there is a graspable Other available for the grasping. What emerges clearly from the Case of the New Orleans Sniper is the range of evidence that may be used to constitute (and unconstitute) an Other. That process is obscured when an Other is unproblematically grasped, but even in such circumstances problems may arise that necessitate the reconstituting or unconstituting of that Other. "Ever new transformations of meaning" remain as possibilities.

I now return to Husserl's claim, cited earlier:

> it is necessary to begin with a systematic explication of the overt and
> implicit intentionality in which the being of others for me becomes
> 'made' and explicated in respect of its rightful content—that is, its
> fulfillment-content (Fifth Cartesian Meditation, 1960: 91–92).

It is just this systematic explication that I have sought here. I have tried to follow Husserl's guidelines in exploring a particular event, one in which an Other is first "made" and then "unmade." Of particular significance is that an Other is indeed "made" and may not stay "made" or stay "unmade." The work of constitution or unconstitution continues.

NOTES

1. Plausibility itself is an ambiguous feature. For some people the existence of ghosts, aliens from outer space, spiritual beings, etc., is plausible while for others the very possibility of such beings is denied.

APPENDIX:
WITNESSES' SIGHTINGS AND DESCRIPTIONS OF SNIPER(S)

As a point of comparison with witnesses' descriptions, police described the body of Mark Essex on the roof of Howard Johnson's as follows:

> Negro male, 5'7", 141 lbs., age 23, dressed in a green long sleeved shirt, black pullover short sleeved shirt, brown leather belt, green jungle (army) fatigue pants with large side pockets, and black military combat boots. Nearby was a .44 magnum Ruger rifle that was determined to have been purchased by Mark Essex.

Data is compiled from Police Report Narrative (an account of the event and investigation), Interviews, and Description of Scenes. Discrepancies among these are noted, e.g. in her interview Hazel Thomas said the photo of Essex "looks something like [him]"; the Narrative said she positively identified a photo of Essex. I have omitted those sightings that were vague or incomplete, e.g., two hotel guests "were unable to give a description of the individual they had seen. . .and could not even say whether the subject was black or white" (81); and "All three stated that Essex was attired in green pants and an unknown shirt. None of the three could identify Mark Essex from photographs. . . " (103).

Tables of sightings are divided as follows:

> A. Before the event at Howard Johnson's and, *after the event*, attributed to Essex

> B. Inside the hotel prior to shootings from the patio: those who had direct contact with sniper(s)

> C. Inside the hotel during the shootings from the patio: a period of somewhat more than an hour during which there was direct contact with sniper(s)

> D. Outside the hotel viewing the patio: observations were made from buildings overlooking Howard Johnson's: Rault Building (Rault Center), Bank of New Orleans Building (also referred to as Gas and Oil Building), Demontluzin

Building, Saratoga Building, Warwick Hotel, and Baronne Building. (The Mayor did not allow police on the roof of City Hall.)

E. Outside the hotel viewing the roof after the patio shootings

F. After Essex's death

Notes on Tables:

Column 1, Time. The order follows the estimates provided in the Narrative Timeline. Times offered by witnesses are included where available. Some witnesses did not offer time estimates but were given them by the interviewer, e.g. "Were you working at the Howard Johnson's on Sunday, January 7, 1973 at approximately 10:45 AM [11:00 AM]?" Entries are chronological only in a general sense, not sighting by sighting.

Column 5, Certainty/Uncertainty. Blank cells indicate no information provided in the Report. It may be that some witnesses were shown photos after their interviews, which would explain the absence of such identification in the interviews themselves, but the Report does not so indicate. Noteworthy discrepancies are highlighted in *italics*.

A. SIGHTINGS BEFORE HOWARD JOHNSON'S AND RETROSPECTIVELY ASSIGNED TO SNIPER(S)

Time & Place	Source	Description	Certainty/Uncertainty
1/1/73 6:30 p.m. First sighting of person who could be sniper First New St. Mark Baptist Church	Rev. Sylvester S. Williams, pastor	Negro male, short hair, early 20s, about 5'6"–7", dark, medium build [narrative says "thin"], about 150 lbs., wearing dark clothing and a dark jacket	Could not identify photos but did say photo of Essex looked similar in height and build; couldn't see face clearly because of poor lighting, not positive of identification
1/2/73 6:00 p.m. Joe's Grocery	Joe Perniciaro, grocer	Negro male, age 20–25, 5"10", 140 lbs., with a small bush hairstyle and light moustache and goatee, wearing army fatigue-type uniform. Had bandage with what appear to be blood stains on left hand.	Refused to identify subject
"	Darryl Davis, grocery clerk	Negro male, age 20–25, 5"10", 150 lbs., small bush hairstyle and light moustache and goatee, bags under his eyes, army clothes, safari-like jacket, pants with large pockets, bandage on hand	Identified photo #48374 (of whom?)
1/7/73 10:30 a.m. Joe's Grocery	Joe Perniciaro, grocer	Refused to give description	Initially indicated that was the same person as on 1/2, but in a later interview stated "that none of his problems would have happened if he had not gone to the police and that he could not identify the subject who had shot him" (PR: 66)

continued

Time & Place	Source	Description	Certainty/Uncertainty
"	Darryl Davis, grocery clerk	Negro male, age 18–19, dark black hair, medium bush, rifle with black barrel and brown handle, 2-1.2–3 feet long	*Said he had never seen person before, i.e., not the same as 1/2*
"	Angela Davis, grocery clerk	Young negro male, about age 17, 5"3", 120 lbs. small afro hair style, medium complexion, black quilted thermo jacket, pink scarf under jacket, green khaki shirt and pants, rifle with black barrel and brown handle 2-1/2–3 feet long, no scope	Report says identified photo of Essex (not mentioned in her interview)
"	Charles Willis, grocery shopper	Black man, medium complexion, age 20–22, 5'2"–3", 125–130 lbs., slim build, medium bush, black jacket and green uniform pants, orange colored scarf hanging from jacket	Did not identify
1/7/73 10:37 a.m. In his car (which was stolen by subject)	Marvin Albert, owner of stolen car	Negro male, 5', 120–125 lbs., slim build, medium bush, medium brown complexion, clean-shaven, sideburns to middle of ear, light green wind-breaker and trousers, looked like .44 magnum.	Shown photo (of Essex?), #48378, "looks like him but is not him." Report says he positively identified a military photograph of Essex.
10:39 a.m. In car hit by Albert's car	Tomar Friedman, accident victim	Negro male, early 20s, light skin, 2" bush, nose not broad, white shirt	

B. SUNDAY 1/7 SIGHTINGS INSIDE HOWARD JOHNSON'S: PRIOR TO PATIO SHOOTINGS

Time & Place	Source	Description	Certainty/Uncertainty
Police estimate: 10:45 a.m. Interview says shortly after 10:00 a.m. Parking garage	Marvin Crosby, parking attendant	Young Puerto Rican or Spanish, not white, perhaps light complected negro, short hair, no hat, alone in the car	
No time given Parking lot, looking into Albert's car	Mr. & Mrs. Billy Joe Palmer and sons Billy Joe, Jr. and Edward, hotel guests	One occupant in car, young Negro male, bush haircut, dark clothes	Mrs. Palmer and Edward identified photo of Essex but said person they saw was lighter
Time given by interviewer 8th floor corridor, looking through door into stairwell	Hazel Thomas, hotel maid (spoke with sniper)	Negro male, age 19–20, brown skin, small bush, brown jacket with revolutionary flag patch on right shoulder, top teeth looked like they were filed	Narrative says positively identified photo of Essex but in interview she says "looks something like" (PR: 829)
Time given by interviewer 8th floor looking through door to stairwell	Carolyn Ardis, hotel maid (spoke with sniper)	Colored male, 20s, short, medium complexion, hair looked uncombed, green fatigue pants, green camouflage-like jacket, pockets of pants were bulging, rifle, with red, green, and black handkerchief around bottom, calm	Did not identify any photo
Interview says 10:30 9th floor	Annie McCoy, hotel maid (spoke with sniper)	Negro male, age 16, 5', thin build, very nappy hair, green fatigue pants (work clothes like dock workers) and gun, perhaps shotgun	Shown one photo (what photo not indicated) and did not recognize him. Narrative states that she said sniper looked like photo but she was not positive.

continued

84   Appendix

Time & Place	Source	Description	Certainty/Uncertainty
Time given by interviewer 18th floor in corridor	Delores Arnold, hotel maid (spoke with sniper)	Negro male, early 20s, 4'11–5', light brown skin, medium length nappy-looking hair, greenish army jacket, short rifle with brown handle	Identified photo (apparently of Essex)
Time given by interviewer 18th floor corridor, subject walking towards Gravier Street stairwell	Eva Mae Washington, hotel inspector	Black male, age 19–20, 5'2"–3", thin build, short hair, green army-like jacket, long rifle	Identified photo of Essex as very similar
10:25–10:30 (heard gunshot) Hall outside 18th floor hotel room, subject leaving hotel room	Margie Lindau, hotel guest	Negro male holding "object" (perhaps gun), medium height, perhaps sunglasses, hat with brim, possibly moustache and beard, jacket similar to leather jacket	
10:30–10:35 (heard shots) Hall outside 18th floor hotel room	Gabe A. Crawford, hotel guest/later interviewed as A.G. Crawford	Negro male with rifle, 5'6"–7", 125–130 lbs., brown skin, medium bush, dark jacket or clothing, neat, regular haircut	Did not identify photo
No time given 11th floor corridor with Frank Schneider (who was killed)	Donald W. Roberts, hotel bellhop	Negro male, 5'8" at most, old clothes, 160–165 lbs, slim build, light complexion, long gun, thought a shotgun	

continued

Appendix

Time & Place	Source	Description	Certainty/Uncertainty
Interview says a little after 10:00 a.m. 11th floor corridor as subject entered from Gravier St. stairwell, later from 10th floor balcony saw him on patio	Beatrice Greenhouse, hotel maid (spoke with sniper)	Negro male, late teens or early 20s, 5'7", medium build, matted hair, no moustache or goatee. (Also saw him on 8th floor patio.)	*Looked like photos #48-374 and 278-255*
Time given by interviewer 11th floor corridor as subject entered from stairwell	Carrie Mae Clemmons, hotel maid (spoke with sniper)	Not dark, could be white or black. Moustache. Color of army clothes on bottom, something on his back (backpack?), "big old long gun"/"big-bellied long gun."	*Photo of Essex NOT the person she saw. From newspaper photos, identified Robert Peters, said she had not seen Essex. Was emphatic.*

C. SUNDAY SIGHTINGS INSIDE HOWARD JOHNSON'S: PATIO SHOOTINGS 10:57 A.M. TO 12:10 P.M.

Time & Place	Source	Description	Certainty/Uncertainty
Between 10:57 a.m. and 12:10 p.m. 8th floor in room overlooking patio	William R. Gillaspy, hotel guest	Light skinned WHITE male, age 20–25, 5'10", 145–150 lbs., green army-type field jacket, possibly jeans, carbine rifle on 30 caliber frame	
Between 10:57 a.m. and 12:10 p.m. 8th floor in room overlooking patio	Carolyn Ann Capel, hotel guest	Black man, medium height, age 23–24, navy blue plain jacket, dark shirt, blue jeans, dark or black shoes, medium afro, average build, no moustache or beard, rifle	One photo resembles subject but cannot be positive. (Narrative says she identified a photo of Essex.) Identified photo of Ruger .44 magnum carbine rifle.
Between 10:57 a.m. and 12:10 p.m. On 8th floor patio, after he was shot by sniper	Robert C. Beamish, injured hotel guest	Negro male, 5'8", rather slim, 165 lbs., low, neatly clipped afro, light colored skin, perhaps a small goatee, light tan jacket or sweater, medium brown trousers, perhaps plaid, bolt action rifle, no scope or sling (not a .44 magnum carbine rifle). Saw subject 4 or 5 times.	*Did not identify any photo (may have said it was not Essex; interview unclear). Seemed to have longest opportunity to observe subject. Rescued by police at 12:57 p.m.*
Between 10:57 a.m. and 12:10 p.m. On 8th floor patio	David F. Moyers, hotel guest	Negro, brown skin, under age 25, 5'5"–8", stocky build, high hair laid down to one side, flat nose, small blue cloth cap, light brown coat buttoned to neck, grey pants, rifle like army carbine.	*Positively identified photo #48376 of Robert Steeward.* *Is this Robert Steward who was later interviewed? (PR: 274ff)*

D. SUNDAY SIGHTINGS OUTSIDE AND OVERLOOKING HOWARD JOHNSON'S: PATIO SHOOTINGS 10:57 A.M. TO 12:10 P.M.

Time & Place	Source	Description	Certainty/Uncertainty
17th floor of Rault Building, overlooking 10th [sic] floor balcony of Howard Johnson's	Odissefs Vrettos, engineer in Rault Building	Two negro male subjects, shorter one with rifle. Unarmed negro male: age 27, 5'10" tall, very light skin, very thin build, medium bush, grey jacket, dark, possibly green pants, large (ammunition?) belt, looked familiar to V.	*Described 2 snipers seen together. Tentatively identified photo of Curtis J. Moss as similar to larger subject but without the moustache and goatee. Said he had seem him before (but hadn't seen Essex before).*
8th floor of Rault Building (overlooking hotel patio)	Odissefs Vrettos, engineer in Rault Building	Saw Beamish shot	Identified (at morgue) Essex as sniper with rifle who shot Beamish; could not identify from photos
From about 11:00–11:10 a.m. (shooting of fireman) On ground outside hotel looking at patio	Police Detective Charles Faught (no interview)	Negro male, saw him shoot Lt. Ursin, fireman	Identified Essex
From about 11:00–11:10 a.m. (shooting of fireman) From sidewalk looking at patio	William James Cooper, hotel guest	Black male, army fatigue pants with large pockets on legs, rifle or shotgun (used pumping motion like it was a pump rifle and shotgun), shot fireman	
From about 11:00–11:10 a.m. (shooting of fireman) From sidewalk looking at patio	Michael J. Knapp, hotel guest	Negro male, shot fireman with rifle, young, dark brown face, dark clothing, all one outfit, top was black or dark blue	

continued

Time & Place	Source	Description	Certainty/Uncertainty
From about 11:00–11:10 a.m. (shooting of fireman) Rault Building, 8th floor looking at patio	Sgt. Donald D. Moore, Sr.	Negro male, black shirt or jacket, either black pants or blue jeans, large bush, 5'9", 150 lbs., rifle or shotgun. Exchanged fire. 30–40 minutes later, saw Negro male, medium bush, olive drab or green clothes, 5'8", 140 lbs. rifle or shotgun.	*Saw Essex's body on rooftop* *Neither male looked like subject seen on roof (Essex)*
From about 11:00–11:10 a.m. (shooting of fireman) First subject: from fire ladder; Second subject: From sidewalk (looking at patio? position unclear)	Police Officer William J. Trepagnier (interview on 1/9)	First subject: Negro male, early 20s, green jumpsuit, thin, rifle with scope. Second subject: Negro male, dark jacket, blue, or black, early 20s, dark skinned, rifle with scope.	*"I think that they were two different people" PR:. 595)*
From about 11:00–1:10 a.m. (shooting of fireman) Sidewalk looking at patio; later looking at 18th floor	Firefighter Louis E. Roussell	Negro male, 20s, 5'9"–10", 155–160 lbs., dark complexion, small bush, zipped-up all-green uniform, shiny clamp at waist; 10 minutes later saw a second, "completely different from the first": Negro male, much lighter complexion, rifle, 6', heavier than other sniper, light brown coat with lighter collar and sleeves, small bush, shot policeman. (617–8)	*Emphatic about descriptions of two sniper*

continued

Appendix

Time & Place	Source	Description	Certainty/Uncertainty
Rault Center, says looking at 10th floor but seems to be describing 8th floor patio	Joseph Victor, employee of Rault Center (in PR, Section M. Rault Center Investigation)	Negro male, age 18–21, 5'4" 125–130 lbs., slim build, blue jacket and possibly blue pants; second negro male subjects: tall, light complexioned, large bush, large belt, unarmed	Identified Essex in morgue; described a second subject
Rault Building, 10th floor overlooking pool	Randal Blanchard, assisting father in duties	Negro male, dark clothing, dark shirt or shirt with dark jacket, age 20s, short afro, black rifle, right hand was trigger hand	
Rault Building, 8th floor looking at patio	Police Officer John Darsam	Colored male, age about 25, tan clothing including tan jacket, rifle	
Rault Building, 8th floor, looking at patio	Police Officer Jessi Stalnaker	Quick view of one subject. Then a negro male, young, light green shirt like a military shirt, unknown trousers, looked like rifle or shotgun.	*Thought the two subjects were different*
From roof, (building not indicated) looking at patio	Police Officer Errol T. Taylor	Blue or dark jacket, dark pants, checkered shirt, 5'10", medium to thin build, dark complected, negro male, age 20's, goatee, rifle	
Demontluzin Building, 10th floor, looking at patio	Officer Robert Zeller	Colored male with rifle, 5'8", full rounded face, short bush, blue jacket and dark clothing underneath	Could not identify photo of Essex

E. SIGHTINGS OUTSIDE AND OVERLOOKING HOWARD JOHNSON'S ROOF: 12:10 P.M. TO ESSEX'S DEATH

Time & Place	Source	Description	Certainty/Uncertainty
Shortly after 12:00 noon Sidewalk by Howard Johnson's looking at 16th floor	Detective William McDonald	Green fatigue-like jacket, medium brown complexion, medium bush, rifle	
1:07 p.m. (timeline estimate; no time given in interview) Warwick Hotel roof looking at H.J. roof	Police Sgt. George Delpidio, Jr.	WHITE, 5'10", rifle, tight-fitting dark blue clothing, short hair. Same person he saw killed on rooftop.	
1:07 p.m. (timeline estimate; no time given in interview) Rault Center roof, looking at H.J. roof (shortly after patio sighting)	Police Officer Edward Griffin	Young, definitely black, boots, fatigue-like clothing, dark in color, medium bush haircut	
3:15 p.m. 18th floor, Bank of New Orleans Building, looking at H.J. roof	Julaine Gray, passerby	Negro male, age unknown, medium bush haircut, large build, perhaps 6', 170 lbs., dark waist-length jacket, knit closures on arms and waist, dark pants, rifle or shotgun	Could not identify photo of Essex and thought subject was larger—but had heard that Essex was 5'4"/135 lbs.

F. MONDAY SIGHTINGS OUTSIDE AND OVERLOOKING HOWARD JOHNSON'S ROOF AFTER ESSEX'S DEATH

Time & Place	Source	Description	Certainty/Uncertainty
3:00 a.m. In Car 114 looking at roof of H.J.	Police Officer Antoine Saacks	"What appeared to be a man" (557-558) or shadow. Was fired at.	
5:00 a.m. Rault Center, 14th floor, looking at H.J. roof	Police Sgt. Ronald Macpherson	Colored male in white shirt on room near cubicle; shot fired at subject?	

BIBLIOGRAPHY
WORKS CITED

ABC News, Vanderbilt University Television News Archive.
   http://tvnews.vanderbilt.edu/
Atkinson, Paul, New Revelation: Did Sniper Start Rault Fire? *The Times-Picayune*, February 16, 1973.
Berryman, Edward (2005) Taking Pictures of Jesus: Producing the Material Presence of a Divine Other, *Human Studies* (28:4) 431–452.
Bourgoyne, J.E., Searched Well, Says Giarrusso, *The Times-Picayune*, January 9, 1973.
CBS News, Vanderbilt University Television News Archive.
   http://tvnews.vanderbilt.edu/
Crider, Bill, Chopper Becomes Flying Gun Platform for Police Riflemen, Associated Press and published in *The States-Item*, January 8, 1973.
Dempsey, Jack, Command Post Grim: Policemen Do Their Duty, Mourn the Fallen, *The States-Item*, January 8, 1973.
——— Sniper Witness Claims He Saw 2 on Balcony, *The States-Item*, January 19, 1973.
Doucet, Clarence, No Trace of Sniper Found after Police Comb Hotel, January 9, 1973.
Goffman, Erving (1963) *Behavior in Public Places: Notes on the Social Organization of Gatherings*, NY: Free Press.
Hernon, Peter (1978/2001) *A Terrible Thunder: The Story of the New Orleans Sniper*, New Orleans, LA: Garrett County. First published by Doubleday, 1978.
Husserl, Edmund (n.d.) Philosophy as Mankind's Self-Reflection: The Self-Realization of Reason, in Edmund Husserl, 1970 (Appendix IV).
——— (before 1928) Idealization and the Science of Reality–The Mathematization of Nature, in Edmund Husserl, 1970 (Appendix II).
——— (1960) *Cartesian Meditations: An Introduction to Phenomenology*, The Hague: Martinus Nijhoff.
——— (1970) *The Crisis of European Sciences and Transcendental Phenomenology: An Introduction to Phenomenological Philosophy*. Tr. with Introduction by David Carr, Evanston, IL: Northwestern University. First published in German, 1954.
——— (1973) *Experience and Judgment: Investigations in a Geneology of Logic*. Revised and edited by Ludwig Landgrebe. Tr. by James S. Churchill and Karl Ameriks. Evanston, IL: Northwestern University. Originally published posthumously in 1948.
Hustmyre, Chuck, Mark Essex, Aftermath.
   http://www.crimelibrary.com/notorious_murders/mass/mark_essex/4.html

Bibliography

Johnson, Allen, Jr., The Heroes of Howard Johnson's, January 7, 2003, *Gambit* website. http://bestofneworleans.com/gyrobase/Content?oid=oid%3A29448

Katz, Allen, A Phantom on the Roof? *The States-Item*, January 9, 1973.

——— Sights, Sounds, Afterthoughts on Sniping, *The States-Item*, January 12, 1973.

——— Did Sniper Aggravate Tensions? Many Say 'No,' *The States-Item*, February 15, 1973.

——— Accomplice Angle Still Up in Air, *The States-Item*, February 20, 1973.

Kifner, John, 'Inside Story' on N.O. Sniper Emerging, *New York Times* and published in *The States-Item*, January 15, 1973.

LaFourcade, Emile, Sniper Rifle Same Used in Other Crimes, *The Times-Picayune*, January 10, 1973.

Lee, Vincent, Police Never Recovered Sniper's Bullet, *The Times-Picayune*, January 12, 1973.

Lincoln, Ray, Violence: Conspiratorial Pattern? *The States-Item*, January 8, 1973.

——— Edwards to Press for Death Penalty, *The States-Item*, January 9, 1973.

Lind, Angus, Wounded Policeman Fears More Deaths, *The States-Item*, January 8, 1973.

——— 2nd Rooftop Sniper or Merely a Ghost? *The States-Item*, January 9, 1973.

——— Mayor Fears 'Sniper 2' Will Remain Mystery, *The States-Item*, January 11, 1973.

MacDonald, George (1869) Uncle Cornelius His Story, in Michael Cox and R.A. Gilbert, *Victorian Ghost Stories* (1991) NY: Oxford University, 130–49.

McMillan, John, Reporters Clearly Heard 'Second Sniper' Shouting, *The Times-Picayune*, January 10, 1973.

——— Deputy Links Sniper, Woman, *The Times-Picayune*, January 12, 1973.

NBC News, Vanderbilt University Television News Archive. http://tvnews.vanderbilt.edu/

Newhouse, Eric, Shot by Second Man—Guest, Associated Press and published in *The Times-Picayune*, January 10, 1973.

——— 2nd Gunman, Victim Insists, Associated Press and published in *The States-Item*, January 10, 1973.

New Orleans (LA) Police Dept. (August 31, 1973) *Report Relating to the Homicide Investigation Conducted into the Criminal Activities of Mark J. Essex, Jr., Age 23, Formerly Residing 2619-1/2 Dryades Street*. From City Archives, Louisiana Division, New Orleans Public Library (PR).

Persica, Dennis, A City Under Siege, *The Times-Picayune*, January 7, 1998.

Rudolph, Maren, Reloading Heard, Firemen Braved Bullets to Battle Sniper Blazes, *The Times-Picayune*, January 12, 1973.

Sheets-Johnstone, Maxine (1996) An Empirical-Phenomenological Critique of the Social Construction of Infancy, *Human Studies* (19:1) 1–16.

——— (1999) Re-Thinking Husserl's Fifth Meditation, *Philosophy Today* (43 Supplement) 99–106.

——— (2003) Child's Play: A Multidisciplinary Perspective, *Human Studies* (19:3) 409–30.

Shibutani, Tamotsu (1966) *Improvised News: A Sociological Study of Rumor*, Indianapolis and NY: Bobbs-Merrill.

Sims, Patsy, Charity Has Its Heroes Too, January 8, 1973.

——— Community Calm Urged, *The States-Item*, January 10, 1973.

States-Item (New Orleans), Snipers Elude Trap on Rooftop of Hotel, January 8, 1973a.

——— City Police Warned of Detroit Gunmen, January 8, 1973b.

——— Mayor Calls for Return to Normality, January 9, 1973a.

—— Hotel Sniper Identified, Terror Shootings Linked, January 9, 1973b.
—— Guest Trapped on Balcony: 'Tried to Make Myself Part of Concrete,' January 9, 1973c.
—— Arson Cases Unrelated, Says Fire Chief, January 9, 1973d.
—— Eastland Sees Plot in Police Killing, January 9, 1973e.
—— Honeymooners Tell of Terror, January 10, 1973a.
—— Police Investigate Sniper 'Conspiracy,' January 10, 1973b.
—— Mayor Fears'Sniper 2' Will Remain Mystery, January 11, 1973.
—— 2 Sniper Rifles? No Evidence Yet, January 12, 1973a.
—— 3 Police Families Receive Donation, January 12, 1973b.
—— He Just Walked Away: At Least 2 Snipers—Fire Chief, January 16, 1973a.
—— Some Information on Sniping Is Being Withheld—Giarrusso, January 16, 1973b.
—— Guste Presses for Plot Probe, January 22, 1973.
—— Hotel Sniper Aided In Arson—Marshal, February 10, 1973.
30 Year Anniversary of NOLA Sniper, December 14, 2002. http://tchouptrack.blogspot.com/2004/09/30-year-anniversary-of-nola-sniper.html
Thomas, Lanny, Background of Sniper Bullet Tests Draw Focus, *The States-Item*, January 10, 1973a.
—— Sniper-Type Weapon is Easy to Purchase, *The States-Item*, January 10, 1973b.
Time, Crime: Death in New Orleans, January 22, 1973. http://www.time.com/time/magazine/article/0,9171,903692,00.html
Times-Picayune (New Orleans), No Trace of Sniper Found After Police Comb Hotel, January 9, 1973a.
—— Hunt for Deadly Sniper Continues, January 9, 1973b.
—— Waving of 'Mystery Man' on Balcony Cleared Up, January 9, 1973c.
—— Autopsy Shows Essex Died of 'Innumerable' Injuries, January 16, 1973.
—— Essex Believed Probably Alone, January 25, 1973.
—— Police Say Lone Sniper Possible, February 20, 1973.
Treadway, Joan, Volunteers Sought, Storming of Hotel Roof Follows Lengthy Vigil, *The Times-Picayune*, January 9, 1973.
Virgets, Ronnie, Fears Don't Fade for Cops Who Recall 1973 Sniper Detail, *The Times-Picayune*, January 11, 1987.
Waksler, Frances Chaput (1987) Dancing When the Music is Over: A Study of Deviance in a Kindergarten Classroom, in Adler, Patricia and Peter (Eds.), *Sociological Studies of Child Development Volume 2*, Greenwich, CN. Reprinted in Waksler, Frances Chaput (Ed.) Studying the Social Worlds of Children, Basingstoke, England: Falmer, 1991, 95–112.
—— (1991) Disembodied Evidence: The Social Significance of Inanimate Phenomena. Paper presented at meetings of Eastern Sociological Society, Providence, Rhode Island, April 1991.
—— (1996) *The Little Trials of Childhood and Children's Strategies for Dealing with Them*. London, England: Falmer Press.
—— (2005) Analogues of Ourselves: Who Counts as an Other? *Human Studies* (28:4) 417–29.

RELATED BIBLIOGRAPHY

In addition to the works cited, an eclectic range of other materials provided important background.

Baker, Carolyn D. and Peter Freebody (1987) Constituting the Child in Beginning School Reading Books, *British Journal of Sociology of Education* (8:1) 55–76.

Barber, Michael (2010) Somatic Apprehension and Imaginative Abstraction: Cairn's Criticisms of Schutz's Criticisms of Husserl's Fifth Meditation, *Human Studies* (33:1) 1–21.

Beavan, Colin (2001) *Fingerprints: The Origin of Crime Detection and The Murder Case That Launched Forensic Science*, NY: Hyperion.

Bugliosi, Vincent with Bruce B. Henderson (1991) *And the Sea Will Tell*, NY: W.W. Norton.

Caplan, Paula J. (1995) *They Say You're Crazy: How the World's Most Powerful Psychiatrists Decide Who's Normal*, Reading, MA: Addison-Wesley.

Carr, David (1970) Translator's Introduction, in Edmund Husserl, 1970, xv–xliii.

Clancy, Susan A. (2005) *Abducted: How People Come to Believe They Were Kidnapped by Aliens*, Cambridge, MA: Harvard University.

Cohen, Howard S. and Michael Feldberg (1991) *Power and Restraint: The Moral Dimension of Police Work*, Westport, CN and London: Praeger.

Crist, Eileen (1999) *Images of Animals: Anthropomorphism and Animal Mind*, Philadelphia: Temple University.

Cuff, E.C. (1994) *Problems of Versions in Everyday Situations*, Washington, DC: International Institute for Ethnomethodology and Conversation Analysis & University Press of America.

de Waal, Frans (2001) *The Ape and the Sushi Master: Cultural Reflections of a Primatologist*, NY: Basic Books.

Garfinkel, Harold (1967) *Studies in Ethnomethodology*, Englewood Cliffs, NJ: Prentice-Hall.

George, Jean Craighead (1985) *How to Talk to Your Dog*, NY: Warner Books.

Ginzburg, Carlo (1982) *The Cheese and The Worms: The Cosmos of a Sixteenth-Century Miller*. Tr. John and Anne Tedeschi, NY: Penguin.

Goffman, Erving (1959) *The Presentation of Self in Everyday Life*, Garden City, NY: Doubleday Anchor.

——— (1974) *Frame Analysis*, NY: Harper & Row.

Goode, David (1994) *A World Without Words: The Social Construction of Children Born Deaf and Blind*. Forward by Irving Kenneth Zola. Phildelphia, PA: Temple University.

Goode, Erich and Nachman Ben-Yehuda (1994) *Moral Panics: The Social Construction of Deviance*, Oxford UK and Cambridge USA: Blackwell.

Grandin, Temple and Catherine Johnson (2005) *Animals in Translation: Using the Mysteries of Autism to Decode Animal Behavior*, NY: Scribner.

Guarnieri, Patrizia (1993) *A Case of Child Murder: Law and Science in Nineteenth-Century Tuscany*, England: Polity. Tr. Claudia Mieville. First published in Italy as L'Ammazzabambini, 1988.

Hahn, Emily (1988) *Eve and the Apes: The Extraordinary History of Nine Women and Their Primates*, NY: Ballantine Books.

Hearne, Vicki (1987) *Adam's Task: Calling Animals by Name*, NY: Alfred A. Knopf.

Husserl, Edmund (1935) The Vienna Lecture, in Edmund Husserl, 1970 (Appendix I).
—— (1962) *Ideas: General Introduction to Pure Phenomenology*, first published in German, 1913, NY: Collier Books.
—— (1964) *The Idea of Phenomenology*, The Hague: Martinus Nijhoff, Trans. William P. Alston and George Nakhnikian.
Kohák, Erazim (1978) *Idea and Experience*, Chicago and London: University of Chicago.
Lane, Harlan (1976) *The Wild Boy of Aveyron*, Cambridge, MA: Harvard University.
Malinowski, Bronislaw (1927) *The Father in Primitive Psychology*, NY: W.W. Norton.
Masson, Jeffrey Moussaieff (1994) *Against Therapy*, Monroe, ME: Common Courage Press, revised edition. First published 1988, NY: Atheneum.
Mead, George Herbert (1964) *Selected Writings*, Indianapolis: Bobbs-Merrill.
—— (1964) *George Herbert Mead On Social Psychology*, Chicago and London: University of Chicago.
Robinson, Wayne A. (1975) *I Once Spoke in Tongues*, NY: Pillar Books. Copyright by author 1973.
Rosenthal, Edith (1997) *Identity as a Collective, Interactional and Occasioned Accomplishment: The Case of Imposture*, Unpublished dissertation, Boston University.
Roth, Julius A. (1957) Ritual and Magic in the Control of Contagion, *American Sociological Review* (22:3) 310–14.
Sacks, Harvey (1989) *Harvey Sacks—Lectures 1964–1965, Special Issue*, Gail Jefferson, ed., *Human Studies*, 12(3–4). Introduction/Memoir by Emanuel A. Schegloff.
Sacks, Oliver (1995) *An Anthropologist on Mars*, NY: Vintage Books, A Division of Random House.
Schutz, Alfred (1964) Don Quixote and the Problem of Reality, in Schutz, 1964, 135–58.
—— (1964) *Collected Papers II: Studies in Social Theory*, edited and introduced by Arvid Brodersen, The Hague, Netherlands: Martinus Nijhoff.
—— (1967) *The Phenomenology of the Social World*. Tr. George Walsh and Frederick Lehnert, n.p.: Northwestern University. First published in German, 1932.
—— (1967b) *Collected Papers I: The Problem of Social Reality*, edited and introduced by Maurice Natanson, The Hague, Netherlands: Martinus Nijhoff.
—— (1967) On Multiple Realities, in Schutz, 1967b, 207–59.
Scott, Marvin B. and Stanford M. Lyman (1968) Accounts, *American Sociological Review* (33:1) 46–62.
Sereny, Gitta (1998) *Cries Unheard: Why Children Kill: The Story of Mary Bell*, NY: Henry Holt.
Sheets-Johnstone, Maxine (1994) *The Roots of Power: Animate Form and Gendered Bodies*, Chicago and LaSalle, IL: Open Court.
Smith, Greg (Ed.) (1999) *Goffman and Social Organization: Studies in A Sociological Legacy*, London and NY: Routledge.
Spiegelberg, Herbert (1965) The Essentials of the Phenomenological Method, The Hague: Martinus Nijhoff, Chapter XIV (Offprint) of Herbert Spiegelberg, *The Phenomenological Movement: A Historical Introduction*, 2nd Ed.
—— (1973) On the Right to Say "We": A Linguistic and Phenomenological Analysis, in George Psathas (Ed.), *Phenomenological Sociology: Issues and Applications*, NY, John Wiley & Sons, 129–56.
Todd, Dennis (1995) *Imagining Monsters: Miscreations of the Self in Eighteenth-Century England*, Chicago and London: University of Chicago.

Waksler, Frances Chaput (1973) *The Essential Structure of Face-to-Face Interaction: A Phenomenological Analysis*, unpublished Ph.D. dissertation.
——— (1995) Introductory Essay: Intersubjectivity as a Practical Matter and a Problematic Achievement, *Human Studies* (18:1) 1–7.
——— (2001) Medicine and the Phenomenological Method, in S.K. Toombs (Ed.), *Handbook of Phenomenology and Medicine*, Dordrecht/ Boston/London: Kluwer Academic Publishers, 67–86. Phenomenology and Medicine Series, Vol. 68.
——— (2005) Analogues of Ourselves: Who Counts as an Other, *Human Studies* (28:4) 417–29.
——— (Ed.) (2005) Thinking About The Other, *Human Studies* Special Issue (28:4).
Wattam, Corinne (1989) Investigating Child Sexual Abuse—A Question of Relevance, in Harry Blagg, John A. Hughes, and Corinne Wattam (Eds.), *Child Sexual Abuse*, England, Longman, 27–43.
Weston, Paul B. and Kenneth M. Wells (1986) *Criminal Evidence for Police*, 3rd Ed., Englewood Cliffs, NJ: Prentice-Hall.

INDEX

air conditioning system, 13, 24, 34, 36, 73
ambiguity, 3–4, 5, 12, 15, 25, 32, 36–37, 60, 64, 76
ammunition, 10, 29, 30, 41, 49, 62, 64–66, 71, 72
  pistol, 49, 66
  See also ballistics evidence
animate organism, 16, 27, 28, 42
anniversaries of New Orleans sniping event, 67–68
appresentation
  See Husserl
assumption, 16, 17, 19, 32, 41, 44, 47, 49, 57, 62, 68, 75
  immediate context for, 9–12
  power of first, 12–13
attribution, 12, 19, 30, 32, 33, 38, 47, 48–49, 58, 62, 65, 68, 76, 77
  of sounds, 25–27, 59
  to second sniper, 26, 28, 64
    See also second sniper
  to single sniper, 6, 12, 28, 42, 49–50, 55, 57, 59, 63, 68

balcony of Howard Johnson's, 22, 38, 46, 52, 54–55
  See also patio
ballistics evidence, 29–30, 39, 46
bullets, 11, 29–30, 39, 62, 63, 64–65, 69
  See also ammunition
bunker of Howard Johnson's (roof), 12, 23–24, 32, 34, 62, 72
Burkart Manufacturing Company, 9, 46, 63, 64

carbine, 29, 38, 72
  See also weapon
Central Lockup, 9, 29, 31, 45, 46, 52, 57, 63–64, 66, 71
certainty
  See Husserl
Charity Hospital, 25, 51, 54
common sense, 5, 9, 13, 17, 18, 25, 36, 37, 59, 75, 77
confusion, 10, 12, 34, 43, 48–49, 55–58, 59, 68, 69
conspiracy theories, 16, 19, 32–34, 65–67
constitution (of Other), 1–5, 9, 13, 16, 19, 43, 44, 75, 78
  See also unconstitution (of Other)
contradictions, 49, 53, 55, 57, 58, 64, 67, 68
  See also evidence, contradictory
  See also Husserl
cultural objects, 28, 31

disembodied evidence, 28–29, 31, 39

escape, 18, 31, 32, 34–36, 43, 69, 70–71, 73, 76–77
evidence 7, 15, 19, 28, 29, 31, 33–34, 42, 44–50, 52, 53, 55, 57, 58, 62, 63–65, 66, 67, 68, 69, 71, 72, 73, 76–78
  ambiguous, 36–37
    See also ambiguity
  ballistics
    See ballistics evidence

evidence (*continued*)
   contradictory, 41–42, 45, 47, 58, 65
   disembodied
      See disembodied evidence
   face-to-face, 21
      See also face-to face interaction
   legitimating, 12, 37–38
   of an Other, 5, 13, 16, 75–78
   of second sniper, 3, 9, 12, 17, 20, 22, 26, 30, 36, 41–43, 45, 68, 69
      See also second sniper
   of senses, 24
   physical, 7, 34, 43, 44, 47, 67
      See also leavings
   sounds, 25–27, 28, 59
      See also sounds
exchanges, 25, 28, 61–62
   See also reciprocity
   See also sounds
existence
   of other, 2, 3–4, 5, 9, 19, 24, 28, 34, 38, 75–77
   of second sniper, 5, 9, 11, 12–13, 15, 19, 22, 24, 26, 30–31, 32, 34, 41, 42, 44, 47, 65, 67, 73
      See also Husserl
      See also nonexistence
experience, 1, 2, 3, 7, 13, 16, 37, 78
   See also Husserl
explanation, alternative, 17, 24, 27, 34, 36–37, 38, 42–43, 47, 52–53, 55, 59, 60

face-to-face interaction, 2, 20, 21, 28, 38, 50
fantasy other, 1–2
Fifth Cartesian Meditation, 1, 4, 16, 27, 28, 42, 50, 78
   See also Husserl
fingerprints, 63–64, 67, 71, 72
firearms
   See weapon
firecrackers, 29, 51, 59, 60, 63–64, 65, 72, 76
firefighters, 7, 12, 15, 17, 21, 41, 43, 52, 56

First New St. Mark Baptist Church, 31, 45, 46, 57, 63, 64, 71

garage of Howard Johnson's, 18, 26, 45, 70, 71
gun
   See weapon
gunfire, 12, 20, 25–28, 32, 36, 59–60, 61

handgun, 22, 25, 30, 49
   See also weapon
harmoniousness, 19, 67, 68
   See also Husserl
hearable
   See sounds
helicopter, 15, 23, 25, 26, 27, 32, 47, 53, 54, 56, 60, 61–62, 76
Hernon, Peter, 5, 10–11, 23, 25, 27, 31, 43, 46, 60
hostages, 12, 13, 53, 57
hotel employees, 7, 18, 20, 38, 41, 50, 52, 73
hotel guests, 7, 13, 20, 30, 32, 38, 41, 47, 50, 53, 57, 65, 67, 68, 69, 73, 77
   statements by, 11, 17, 18, 21, 25, 30, 37, 45–46, 52, 55, 56, 69–71, 72, 75, 76
hotel maids, 13, 20–21, 35, 46, 47, 50, 51, 56–57
Howard Johnson's Motel
   See balcony, bunker, garage, patio, roof, stairwell
Husserl, Edmund, 1, 3–4, 7, 15, 16, 27–28, 41, 42, 49, 50, 67, 73, 78
   appresentation, 19, 41–42
   certainty, 42
   contradiction, 49
   evidence, 15, 42
   existence, 41–42
   experience, 1, 3, 16, 27, 41–42, 49, 67
   harmoniousness, 42, 67
   illusion, 3, 42
   immanent data, 42
   intentionality, 4, 78
   other, 1, 3, 4, 16, 27, 42, 49, 50, 78

Husserl, Edmund (*continued*)
   physical things, 3, 16
   pseudo-organism, 41–42
   relativity, 3, 49
   sphere of ownness, 16

illusion
   See Husserl
immanent data
   See Husserl
improvised news, 32
intentionality, 28
   See also Husserl
interactional availability
   See face-to-face interaction

Joe's Grocery, 31, 46, 57–58, 63, 64–65, 68, 69, 71

kinetic/tactile-kinesthetic body, 16, 76

leavings, 16, 28–32, 34, 47, 49, 63–65, 68
legitimation, 12, 37–38

mannequin, 1, 7, 77
militants, 12, 13, 32–34, 43–44
movement, bodily, 16, 19, 55, 73, 76

New Orleans Police Department Report, 5, 7, 19, 21, 38, 39, 43–49, 51–59, 61–62, 64–73
New Year's Eve
   See Central Lockup
nonexistence, 9, 28, 41, 75
   See also existence

Oliver Van Horn Company, 46, 63
Other, 1–5, 7, 9, 13, 16–17, 19, 20, 24, 25, 27, 28, 34, 36, 38, 42, 44, 50, 55, 57, 59–60, 73, 75–78
   See also Husserl

path
   for Essex, 46, 63–65,
   for second sniper, 68, 71–73
   See also second sniper
patio of Howard Johnson's, 13, 21, 22, 38, 46, 52–53, 55, 56, 72, 73
   See also balcony
phenomenology, 1, 45, 67
photographs (for identification of sniper), 20–22, 38, 45–46, 50–52, 57, 58, 68, 72
physical things
   See Husserl
physical laws, 17, 76–77
police on the scene, 10, 69, 72
pseudo-organism, 41
   See also Husserl
public safety, 41, 66

Rault Building (Rault Center), 22, 26–27, 33, 52, 54, 56–57, 61, 73
reciprocity, 19, 27–28, 61–62
reformulation, 9, 15, 18, 50, 55, 61–62, 75, 76
reinterpretation, 9, 42–43, 54, 59, 60, 61
relativity of experience
   See Husserl
reliability (of witnesses)
   See witness reliability
revolver, 31, 63, 71
   See also weapon
rifle, 19, 23, 25, 26–27, 29–30, 38, 39, 45–49, 52, 55, 57, 60, 63, 64–65, 68, 72
   See also weapon
roof of Howard Johnson's, 4, 11, 12–13, 15, 19–20, 23–27, 29, 30, 32, 34– 37, 47, 50, 53–54, 56, 59–60, 62, 64, 65, 72, 76, 77
Ruger, 29, 38, 72
   See also weapon

Second Cartesian Meditation, 3
  See also Husserl
second sniper, 3–5, 7, 9, 11–13, 15–20, 22–32, 34–36, 38, 41–47, 49–55, 57, 59, 61–62, 64–73, 75–77
  two snipers together, 22, 25, 32, 50, 52, 68
    See also attribution, evidence, existence, path, traces
seeable
  See sights
Sheets-Johnstone, Maxine, 7, 16, 19, 76
shotgun, 30, 51, 61, 72
  See also weapon
sightings of sniper(s), 10, 19–24, 25–26, 30, 32, 34, 36, 45–46, 47, 50–58, 60, 63–65, 67–69, 71–73, 77
  retrospective sightings, 50, 57–58, 63
sights, 9, 16, 19, 47, 49, 60, 75
skill of sniper(s), 18, 48–49, 64, 73
social change, 33
social framework, 9
social construction, 15, 38
social possibilities, 77
social world, 29
sounds, 9, 16, 19, 25–27, 47, 49, 59–61, 75, 76
  See also voices
speculation, 9, 16, 19, 30, 32–34, 35, 47, 48, 49, 55, 62, 65–67
sphere of ownness
  See Husserl
stairwell of Howard Johnson's, 12, 20–21, 23, 26, 32, 35, 45, 46, 47, 54, 56, 59, 60–62, 69, 76

stolen car, 10, 18, 45, 58, 71
supernatural other, 2

Thomas, W.I., 2
Third Cartesian Meditation, 15, 42
  See also Husserl
timeline of event, 6, 33, 69
traces (of second sniper), 4, 30, 45, 47, 67–71, 73
  See also evidence
  See also second sniper
trial run, 47–48, 75
turn-taking
  See reciprocity

unconstitution (of Other), 3, 5, 9, 19, 27, 41, 44, 45, 47, 49, 51, 53–54, 60–61, 67, 73, 77–78
  See also constitution (of Other)
unreliability (of witnesses)
  See witness unreliability

voices, 15, 25–27, 47, 59, 76
  See also sounds

weapon (firearms, gun), 18, 21, 23, 24, 25, 28, 29–30, 48, 49, 51, 52, 54, 55, 56, 57, 60, 65, 70, 72
  See also handgun, shotgun
witness, 7, 19–20, 22, 31, 35, 38, 41, 45, 50–55, 58, 60–61, 62, 64–65, 66–68, 71–72,
  reliability, 19–20, 22, 24, 36, 37, 38, 58, 67, 77
  unreliability, 19–20, 58, 67, 77

About the Author

Dr. Frances Chaput Waksler, Professor Emerita of Sociology, Wheelock College, is an internationally known phenomenological sociologist and theorist. She received her Ph.D. from the Boston University Department of Sociology. Her books include *The Little Trials of Childhood and Children's Strategies for Dealing with Them* (1996) and the edited volume *Studying the Social Worlds of Children* (1991), both published by Falmer. Her published articles include "Analogues of Ourselves: Who Counts as an Other?," "Medicine and the Phenomenological Method," "Dancing When the Music is Over: A Study of Deviance in a Kindergarten Classroom," "Studying Children: Phenomenological Insights," and, with Professor George Psathas, "The Essential Features of Face-to-Face Interaction." She has served as Associate Editor of the journal *Human Studies*, for which she edited special issues including one entitled *Thinking about the Other*. She is a member of the Society for Phenomenology and Existential Philosophy, the Society for Phenomenology and the Human Sciences, and the Eastern Sociological Society and has presented numerous papers at their meetings.

www.ingramcontent.com/pod-product-compliance
Lightning Source LLC
Chambersburg PA
CBHW031554300426
44111CB00006BA/311